D0782338

C

THE NATURE OF CIVILIZATIONS

EXTENDING HORIZONS BOOKS

THE BLACK POWER REVOLT
edited by Floyd B. Barbour

SOCIAL WORK AND SOCIAL CHANGE
by Sugata Dasgupta

THE DEFINITION OF DEFINITION
by Ralph Borsodi

DEMOCRACY AND NONVIOLENCE
by Ralph T. Templin

THE INTEGRATION OF HUMAN KNOWLEDGE
by Oliver Reiser

THE AMERICAN SEX REVOLUTION
by Sorokin

MARRIAGE: PAST AND PRESENT
by Robert Briffault and Malinowski

NEW TITLES 1969

THE NEW LEFT: A COLLECTION OF ESSAYS
Priscilla Long, Ed. Introduced by Staughton Lynd

MARX & KEYNES: THE LIMITS OF THE MIXED ECONOMY
by Paul Mattick.

VALUES IN HUMAN SOCIETIES
by F. R. Cowell.

THE NATURE OF CIVILIZATIONS

by Matthew Melko

INTRODUCTION

by Crane Brinton

WINGATE COLLEGE LIBRARY

Extending Horizons Books

 Porter Sargent Publisher

Copyright © 1969 by F. Porter Sargent

Library of Congress Catalog Card Number 69-15527

Standard Book Number 87558-044-0

PORTER SARGENT PUBLISHER 11 Beacon St. Boston Mass. 02108

To Martin Wight

49355

Acknowledgments

In 1968 four scholars died, each of whom had a different kind of relationship to the study of comparative history. They will be missed.

Pitirim Sorokin was a comparative historian on the grand scale: he tackled with salty brilliance the task of making sense of history as a whole. "Thus far, history has followed the course I have set for it," he once remarked in a footnote. And in response to a critic he snapped: "Let anyone who can do better, do better; unfortunately so far no one has." Rushton Coulborn was the kind of comparative historian who preferred to work with meticulous care on particular recurrent phenomena: feudalism, the relations of church and state, the origins of civilization. His knowledge of Eastern civilizations surpassed that of any other comparative historian and it is a great loss that he did not live to complete a synthetic study. Crane Brinton was a narrative historian who harnessed and clarified some of the major themes of history. He believed that there should be many approaches to historical problems and he strongly encouraged the interaction of comparative and narrative approaches. Harold Davis was a teaching historian. He read all kinds of history voluminously, and led his students to develop an eye for the broader question or the comparable problem. He breathed, enlarged and transmitted the atmosphere that had been created by the Sorokins, Coulborns and Brintons.

All four had an impact on this book. Sorokin's social philosophy permeates the theoretical skeleton; Coulborn spent his last months at my college during a period when he was giving considerable thought to the development of comparative history as a discipline; Brinton read and criticized the manuscript and, though he was suffering from what proved to be a fatal illness, was kind enough to write an introduction for it; Davis read the manuscript at an earlier stage and acted as a sounding board while the final draft was being written.

Acknowledgments are also due to my wife, who endured a three-year exile while materials were gathered and directions found; to Kenneth Thompson and Frederick L. Schuman for providing early inspiration; to Downing Bowler, Hayden White, Osmo Heila and Mark Carroll for their comments on the manuscript; to Mrs. Harold Johnson, Cre Wilsey Cunniff and Molly Noyes for help in its preparation; to Senay Goker Gulmez who, among many other things, drafted, glued and struggled with the charts of chapter five; to Richard Newman who designed the cover; to the editors of *Main Currents in Modern Thought,* who published an earlier version of chapter one (Jan-Feb. 1965) ; to my editor, Esther Doughty, who has forced me to make this a tighter, clearer, better-organized book. But there never would have been a manuscript to criticize, type or edit if it had not been for the guidance of Martin Wight.

It goes without saying that the people mentioned in the preceding paragraph, having done so much already, will cheerfully share the blame for any shortcomings the book may have, so that none of the responsibilities are mine.

1969   *Matthew Melko*

INTRODUCTION

As the familiar story of Gibbon contemplating the ruins of Rome and resolving on the spot to undertake his *Decline and Fall* illustrates, historians are usually quite aware of the facts of the life and death of *something;* and they do attempt to explain these life-courses in terms of causality. Arnold Toynbee's reproachful "antinomians" is thus not wholly fair towards even the most pedestrian narrative historian. But it is true that the life-courses, the cycles of ups and downs that they recount, and indeed often analyze in a quite respectably scientific manner, are those of a specific political entity, one that can be mapped, firmly located and confined in space and time. The city-states of the ancient world, the nation-states of the modern world, even feudal entities like Bavaria or Brittany, though their boundaries are rarely wholly fixed for long at a time, nonetheless deserve that favorite adjective of the rigorous social scientists — "hard." They are not quite as hard as an individual human being, but they can be fixed, delimited, in a sense isolated. It is true that they have relations among themselves, studied with care and skill as far back as Thucydides. But diplomatic, military, economic and nowadays intellectual historians still work with definable territorial political entities. Such a subject as the influence on the early French revolutionists of the bills of rights of the first state constitutions of the new American republic may seem fuzzy to the radical reductionist, but it can be documented and defined.

But, though they certainly do not refrain from using them, historians for the most part shy off from attempts at close definition of such terms as "civilization," "culture," "society," a task they tend to leave to the anthropologist or the sociologist. And, though there are plenty of text books on the history of Western civilization, or just of civilization, though world history is provided in great and unusually indigestible amounts, these are rarely true comparative histories of civilizations. So distinguished and adventurous a comparative historian as Cyril

Black, for instance, though he is concerned with a subject which cuts across something much broader than the "parochial" nation state, to use Toynbee's loaded word, nevertheless does not think that "civilization" is for the historian a viable working reality.

Yet the attempt to chart, analyze, explain the development of units of wider scope than the political "sovereign" state goes back a long way, at least to St. Augustine and Orosius. Someone somewhere christened this effort the "philosophy of history," a hybrid term distrusted by both philosopers and historians, and contemptuously dismissed as meaningless or worse by conventional social scientists. Frank E. Manuel has traced briefly in his *Shapes of Philosophical History* the history of this kind of history — for history it is — with admirable scholarship, some sympathy, and no more than a decent degree of skepticism. In view of the intellectual gifts of many of those who have turned to this kind of history, the utter scorn poured on it by most historians is not easily explained. Certainly the whole spirit of modern academic historians, duly organized in national associations, has from the start abjured the kind of generalization the philosopher of history has to make. Ranke, their founder, in an often quoted preface, wrote in pride rather than the humility his rhetoric implied that he would not attempt to explain the course of history, but would "merely (*bloss,* really the key word) show what actually happened." The late H.A.L. Fisher, in a preface that annoyed Toynbee very much, made a similar statement: he wouldn't really try to make sense out of history, that great if fascinating series of puzzles.

No doubt the eighteenth and nineteenth century practitioners of what the Enlightened called "philosophic history," a Condorcet, a Comte, a Buckle, were too innocently rationalist expounders of a simple stadial and unilinear theory of progress, and much too exclusively concerned with what is now commonly — very commonly — styled "Western civilization." The same reproach cannot be leveled at their twentieth century successors, Spengler, Toynbee, nor even, and in spite of his ambitious attempts at quantification (towards which Matthew Melko is in this book a bit too kind), Sorokin. These writers, though not even Spengler quite discards the logic of induction, do indeed rely on the hunch, the imaginative leap from the ground of facts to a theory, a generalization, a hypothesis which gets too far off the ground.

They are in a position analogous in many ways to that of the practitioners of another and not totally dissimilar genre, the study of the national character. There surely is such a character, indeed real enough to be called a "thing"; but when, for example, Salvador de Madariaga from the "fact" that the Latin *honor, furor,* became in French *honneur, fureur,* with that feeble, pursed sound of *eu,* but the Latin *amor* becomes *amour,* with that fine full passionate vowel *oo,* — when from this de Madariaga concludes that love is more important to Frenchmen than honor, he is surely hanging too much on too little. Toynbee himself is full of bright ideas, often deserving that golden word, "insights," but also often quite unverifiable; and on the largest scale of generalization, Sorokin's stadial formula of ideational-ideal-sensate is hard to reconcile with continuities clear to a historian.

Matthew Melko in his book is consciously striving to avoid the reproaches of those who maintain that this kind of history is hopelessly removed from the whole way of thinking adequately if not fully exemplified by what we all understand, or think we understand, as the method of natural science. He has of course predecessors, to whom he fully acknowledges his debt. The most important of these are the late Alfred Kroeber and the late Rushton Coulborn. Kroeber was a professional anthropologist whose early training and studies of the California Indians had been impeccably scientific. He developed an interest in the growth — and decay — of what he called "cultures." His *Configurations of Culture Growth* is indeed tentative, undogmatic, worthy of the respect of any scientific investigator. Coulborn, himself an admirer and disciple of Kroeber, and a well-trained professional historian, addressed himself in his later years to precisely this problem of defining "civilizations" and demarcating the confusing boundaries among "civilizations," "societies" and "cultures." Matthew Melko is in this book the legitimate heir of these two distinguished scientists.

He is no mere epigone, however. He has his own style, his own gait, as the reader will discover at once. He has the necessary degree of skepticism, but also the necessary degree of animal faith. He is on occasion colloquial — perhaps, in the eyes of the conventionally detached scientist, undignified. None of his co-practitioners in the field have this same earthy touch, this good humor underlain by genuine modesty; the philosophy of history, it must be admitted, tends towards a certain high seriousness, not to say stuffiness. Melko's relatively brief bibliography and critical comments offer the reader as a bonus a most valuable survey of the field as it is today.

It is a field that will continue to be cultivated in spite of the fact that there are many who regard it as ground that can never yield a profitable crop. For it would seem that far into the forseeable future the great majority of human beings will be incapable of complete scientific skepticisms, will need answers to such questions as "Whither Mankind?" — and "Whither I?" The mysteries, miracles and revelations of the higher religions all give answers to such questions. Once the supernatural bases of these religions are rejected, however, the only available source of answers is the long course of history — history which includes geophysics, historical geology, archaeology, anthropology, and prehistory. (It must be re-iterated that simply *not to ask* such questions is at this moment in cultural evolution just not humanly possible for many people.)

A great deal of work has in the last two centuries or so gone into the effort to wrest from history alone what must be called a religion. Frank Manuel's "Prophets of Paris," from Turgot to Comte, were all concerned in the task. But at the moment it looks as though the only really successful prophet in the sense of converting masses of men is Karl Marx. Marxism is still active, growing, alive; Comtean Positivism is dead, was in fact still-born. Other modern clusters of ideas and emotions with holds over men, and with some institutional form — nationalism, democracy of the "free world" variety, Fascism, Nazism — perhaps because none have made the clean break from Christianity, Islam, or another higher or lower religion — have not really succeeded in achieving a cosmology and eschatology.

As a literary or at least cultural genre, the field we are concerned with is far wider than the institutional and political embodiments discussed above. The classical philosophers of history of our time, Spengler, Toynbee, Sorokin, Quigley and others, of course figure here. There are more specialized and usually less long-winded approaches, such as that of the scientists, more commonly biologists or demographers, concerned with the plundering of our planet, the population explosion, the tampering with nature's (tricky word!) ecological balance; the now rather old-fashioned unilinear cultural evolutionists of Prog-

ress: the seekers after a Western nirvana, such as Roderick
Seidenberg in his *Post-Historic Man;* the neo-Stoics, such as
Charles Galton Darwin, author of *The Next Million Years;* and
finally, at the moment in the height of fashion, which one hopes
will prove duly fickle, the Marshall McLuhan who sees salvation
in what he calls the media.

There remains the little corner of the field that Matthew
Melko, following Kroeber and Coulborn, is here cultivating.
He is trying to cultivate this corner by methods not inconsonant
with those that have borne good crops in both the natural and
the social sciences. These are not cut-and-dried methods, above
all not methods identical for any and all researches. It is a field
that needs a lot of preliminary clearing, which is just what
Melko is doing. May he, in turn, have his followers in the field.
For his is the one approach consonant with the long tradition
of rationalism, realism, or blessed word, science.

Peacham, Vermont   *Crane Brinton*
July, 1968

CONTENTS

LIST OF FIGURES

I

THE CONCEPT OF CIVILIZATIONS

1: THE NEED FOR A MODEL

Valiant attempts to define and describe giant cultures have
become familiar in the twentieth century. Spengler, Toynbee,
Sorokin and Kroeber have each offered impressive systems involving the conception of a number of exclusive, durable, mortal
macrocultures that have come to be called "civilizations." That
these attempts have aroused considerable interest derives, no
doubt, from a feeling that our own civilization might be facing
the possibility of coming to an end, of "dying" if you will, as
others apparently have in the past.

But most scholars, while praising the authors for their learning and audacity, have raised central questions about the validity
of the whole approach. Do these civilizations, ranging over
thousands of miles and years, really have meaningful internal
relationships? Should anyone attempt to characterize them as
if they were historical personalities? Is it possible to unravel
the maze of history and compartmentalize it in this fashion?
And if a Spengler or Toynbee does all this, has he discovered
anything real or has he only found a way of simplifying history
that happens to be convenient for him?

The answers given to these questions, at the time they were
raised, were overwhelmingly negative. The civilizations of

Spengler and Toynbee behaved themselves so beautifully because they were fictitious creations. Since they were not real, they could not live or die and they certainly could not have personalities.

But time has given a different answer. Many historians write today with a sharpened awareness of cultural integration and characterization. They seek relationships between politics, economics and aesthetics, and they dismiss cause-and-effect political history as out of date, something that belongs to the nineteenth century. What they have rejected in the system builders is their dogmatic periodization. The basic concepts have stood. Civilizations do have meaningful inner relationships, they can be characterized, they can be distinguished from one another.

In the last year of his life, Rushton Coulborn wrote that a task "of pressing importance for the comparative study of civilized societies . . . is the establishment of an outline body of doctrine for the whole field secure enough for all scholars working within it to accept." In the essay that follows I hope to make a beginning on the task this thoughtful scholar believed to be so important. I have tried to sift out the areas of agreement that exist among the students of comparative history who, together, have studied most of the civilizations of the world. What, from these areas of agreement, seem to be the recurrent, the usual, the normal characteristics of most civilizations? What is a normal civilization?

Coulborn liked to apply Thomas Kuhn's term, paradigm, to a body of doctrine accepted by almost everyone working within a given field. What I am attempting here, of course, might be called a model of civilization. Others may modify this, or propose alternatives. Out of this kind of interaction, a paradigm for the study of civilization could arise.

Let me stress again that most of the generalizations in this essay are drawn from the observations of comparative historians, and not from an exhaustive study of history itself. In fact, because I do not have an adequate general knowledge of many civilizations, I have tried to set aside my own observations of history or at least to relegate them to the notes. It will, however, be necessary to illustrate some points with examples, which I shall draw from my knowledge of Chinese, Russian, Indian, Egyptian and Western history.

ON NOTES

I have always regarded footnotes with mixed emotions. I hate those little numbers [17] that make you look to the bottom of the page and lose the train of the argument. On the other hand, sometimes I do want to know more about a particular subject and every so often the footnote turns out to be worth more than the argument itself. Also I sometimes want to know where I can read further on a subject or to learn where the author got such bilge in the first place.

So there are no little numbers in the text, and a reader can go from chapter to chapter without any reference to the notes at all. The notes are arranged according to chapter sections or subjects, so that the reader may pause, if he chooses, only at those sections which are of particular concern to him.

The sources are listed at the end of each chapter. They are included in order to tell the reader where he may find more that is interesting, useful or informative on specific subjects he may want to know more about. I have generally confined myself to comparative historians, and have tried to include only those sections that are sufficiently rewarding to be worth the trouble looking up, and to indicate to the reader what he will find in compensation for his efforts.

NOTES

a. Comparative History

I use this term to refer to the study of recurrent phenomena in different civilizations. It isn't a very good term because comparative studies can be made within a single civilization and because it doesn't necessarily involve the writing of history so much as the combining of history, sociology, anthropology and philosophy, with other disciplines sprinkled in according to the capabilities and intentions of the authors. It is to be distinguished from the universal narrative histories of H. G. Wells or William McNeil in that the latter are only incidentally comparative (but indisputably history), and from the philosophies of history of the Hegelian type, since these draw on historical comparisons to prove a specific thesis rather than focusing on the civilizations themselves.

Other terms that have been suggested for what I am calling comparative history are social philosophy (Pitirim Sorokin), culture history (A. L. Kroeber) and analytical history (Carroll Quigley). Each term has its weaknesses, but I should be happy to settle for any of them, if most everyone else would too.

---

[17] and when you do look it usually says *ibid.* 114 or something equally useless or baffling.

b. The Reality of Civilizations

Are civilizations real? Do they exist? Are we discussing examples of
objective reality or are these merely classifications that happen to be convenient for some social philosophers? The assertion that these civilizations
are only matters of convenience, only imaginative fictional constructions,
has led critics to dismiss their study as arbitrary and unscientific, and has
led some comparative historians to have qualms about making insufficiently
supported generalizations.

Perhaps the answers to these questions depend on individual conceptions
of the nature of reality. Civilizations have physical relationships and psychic
relationships; they look different from different viewpoints of time and
space. But this is also true of concepts of space, like Europe, or time, like
the age of Louis XIV. It is also true of material objects. Is a wall real? Is
Hadrian's Wall real? Which Hadrian's Wall? It was a road to the soldier
who walked on it, a policy to Hadrian. For the tourist it is something to
be remembered; for the student it is something to be memorized. It is a
mark of phase to Toynbee, a surface to walk on for a bug, a universe for a
molecule within one of the stones.

Is a matter of convenience real? Is a fictional creation real? Is Hamlet
real? Is Donald Duck real? Are they less real than the United States Secretary of Commerce? I know the Secretary of Commerce is real because I
have seen his picture in the paper. But then I have seen Donald Duck's
picture too. Rather more often.

Reality consists of both physical and psychic relationships, varying in
emphasis depending on whether an observer is within or outside the phenomenon observed. Civilizations have both physical and psychic reality. Most
of them are nebulous, it is true, but no one denies the reality of nebulae.
It is not therefore likely that any one delineation of civilizations will hold
for all time and for all observers. Kroeber suggested that the whole concept
of civilizations may only be an intermediate way of looking at a problem,
and that the next generation may come along with a different macrocultural
concept that proves to be more meaningful. Hence the 'civilization' is only
a researcher's tool; it might be replaced by something else. Or, as G. M.
Young said, it might only be "what the Germans, in their terse and spark-
ling way, call the hypostatization of methodological categories." The destruction of theories of civilizations, however, will not destroy the civilizations themselves.

I think, then, that we can find value in the concept of civilizations without worrying too much about their "reality." They exist within many
contexts and they are relevant to the kind of thinking that is characteristic
of the twentieth century. We can distinguish them, we can characterize
them, and we can find enough parallels in their behavior to generalize about
their development and even to cast these generalizations into a working
model.

2: COMPARATIVE HISTORIANS

Each civilization has a history of its own. We might, therefore, refer to those who have considered the history of one civilization in relation to the history of others as comparative historians.

There have been quite a few comparative historians through the centuries: Orosius, Ibn Khaldun, Bodin, Le Roy, Vico, Danilevsky, Burckhardt, Brooks and Henry Adams. But there is no doubt that the twentieth century crisis of the two world wars, coupled with significant developments in the methods of archaeology and anthropology, cleared the way for the emergence of the most knowledgeable and interesting comparative historians who have ever lived. Of these the most influential have been Spengler, Toynbee, Sorokin and Kroeber.

Oswald Spengler, an obscure German schoolmaster, began his *Der Untergang des Abendlandes* as an effort to comprehend the political events that preceded the First World War. Eventually he enlarged his original scope, believing that politics could only be understood in relation to artistic and philosophical developments. His book is primarily a comparison of Western and Greco-Roman civilizations, with side glances at half-a-dozen others. He is dogmatically insistent on the independence of civilizations from external influences. He writes with leaping flashes of intuition which may be exciting, inspiring, annoying or baffling. His book has been translated by C. F. Atkinson as *The Decline of the West* (London, Allen and Unwin, 1932).

The British historian, Arnold Toynbee, began publishing *A Study of History* (London, Milford, 1934-61) a few years before the outbreak of World War II. Toynbee draws from a wider knowledge of history than Spengler, documents his material more thoroughly, and has at his command an astonishing amount of information on numerous and disparate subjects. He delineates more than twenty civilizations, though even for him Western and Classical civilizations provide the core of his support. He is less concerned than Spengler with characterizing civilizations, more concerned with the criteria by which they are to be determined. The *Study* is both pleasing and exhausting because of its winding side-paths, many carried to footnotes and annexes, where they often lead to observations more significant than the point they are illustrating.

As Toynbee worked steadily on his staggering one-man task, Russian-born Pitirim Sorokin mobilized a small army of Harvard graduate students to help him tackle similar questions from a sociological viewpoint. He concentrates even more than Spengler and Toynbee on the Classical-Western tradition. His *Social and Cultural Dynamics* (New York, American Book Company, 1937-41, 4 vols.; abridged ed., Boston, Porter Sargent, 1957) overflows with statistics on all conceivable components of a culture, from types of art and systems of truth to methods of government and practice of war. Sorokin and his students have not only studied them, they have tried to weigh and measure them. Basing his writing on these data, Sorokin is often difficult to read. Fortunately his books are salted with pugnacious overtones, particularly in the footnotes. Though a harsh critic of his fellow comparative historians, he is also a staunch defender of what they are trying to do.

A. L. Kroeber, born four years before Spengler, did not publish his *Configurations of Culture Growth* (Berkeley, University of California Press, 1944) until the latter part of World War II (though it was virtually completed nearly a decade earlier). Kroeber is more temperate and less conclusive than the others. He suggests areas for further investigation without trying to supply final answers to his own questions. He has consistently attempted to reconcile conflicting views of his fellow writers in the field without interpreting them, as Sorokin tends to do, in his own terms. He approaches civilizations from an anthropological viewpoint, seeing them as more complex, but not magically different, from simpler cultures. He is the most comfortable of the four in dealing with non-Western cultures. He writes in a mellow style, sometimes over-elaborated by his anxiety to qualify and avoid overstatement.

A number of other twentieth-century scholars have made significant contributions to comparative history.

The British egyptologist, Flinders Petrie, anticipated Spengler and Toynbee in his bold, scarcely-supported speculations about the nature and development of civilizations, the relations between them and the nature of progress. Christopher Dawson, British Catholic historian, approaches the subject as a student of comparative religion, avoids constructions of central theories and, like Kroeber, stresses the importance of intermediate cultures. Quincy Wright, drawing heavily on Toynbee for theoretical support, concentrates on the structures of international societies. Shepard Clough focuses on the relationship between the development of civilizations and their economic system. Philip Bagby, an American anthropologist, outlined methods and suggested studies that ought to be undertaken in comparative history, but his early death prevented him from completing any significant study of his own.

Two other comparative historians, writing more recently, have made important contributions. Rushton Coulborn concentrated on the origin and revival of civilizations. He stressed the tendency of civilizations to endure and recover, the importance of "style" in determining their delineation, and the necessity of remaining receptive to partial comparisons ("uniformities") without imposing a rigid, overall structure. Carroll Quigley has written a concentrated, sophisticated explanation of *The Evolution of Civilizations* (New York, Macmillan, 1961). His style is simple, direct and often humorous; he is particularly concerned about explaining the correlation in the development of psychic, governmental and economic aspects of a civilization. Coulborn and Quigley represent a new generation: their tools are more refined than those of their predecessors, and they are less dogmatic. Perhaps because they have been in a position to support themselves with more certainty they are less outrageous and have therefore attracted less attention. This is unfortunate, because they have much to say and there is still much to be said.

3: How Civilizations Are Integrated

The term "culture" is used to describe the way men live in relation to one another. Sometimes the culture may be simple and complete, easy to understand as a whole, as is frequently the case with the island cultures studied by anthropologists.

Civilizations are large and complex cultures, usually distinguished from simpler cultures by a greater control of environment, including the practice of agriculture on a large scale and the domestication of animals. They are technically advanced enough to use metals and to employ the wheel for transportation. These economic advantages give them enough of a surplus of food and necessities to free some of their members, at least in part, from subsistence work. This freedom usually leads to the building of cities, and the development of more complex art forms and some kind of writing to convey ideas and to maintain records. For whereas a simpler culture changes so slowly that it is usually studied in static terms, a civilization changes rapidly enough to be considered chronologically: it has a history (Quigley, *The Evolution of Civilizations,* pp. 69-76).

Usually civilizations incorporate a multiplicity of cultures and languages. But they have never expanded indefinitely, and it has been possible to distinguish them not only from their component cultures, but also from other civilizations. When Marco Polo traveled to China, he was aware that he was seeing a distinct civilization. The Chinese and Europeans each lived their own lives, and contact between them was rare. There was no society which included Europe and China. They were clearly separate entities. The geographical distinction is not always so clear, but civilizations that form and develop separately tend to remain distinct even after they come into physical contact.

Toynbee sums up the incorporative but distinct characteristics of civilizations when he describes them as institutions that "comprehend without being comprehended by others" (*A Study of History,* I: p. 455, n. 1).

These civilizations must have a certain degree of integration. Their parts are defined by their relationship to each other and to the whole. If the civilization is composed of states, these states will have more relation to one another than they do to states outside the civilization. They might fight more, and engage more frequently in diplomatic relations. They will be more interdependent economically. There will be pervading aesthetic and philosophical currents.

The degree of integration that exists will vary from one civilization to another and it will vary within a civilization from time to time. Sometimes the parts will be so closely related that a change in one part will affect all the others, both geographically and in terms of ideas and attitudes. Sometimes the parts will be loosely related, so that a change in one part will have very little effect on the others. These degrees of integration are familiar in other systems. If you pull a man out of a football team, you still have a team that works, less efficiently perhaps, but it does work and is still clearly identifiable as the same team. If you knock a neutron out of an atom you get an isotope with considerably different properties. Similarly, the Polish Partition involved the removal of a state, but still the system worked, less efficiently perhaps, but it did work and was clearly identifiable as the same state system. But the Reformation involved a replacement of qualities so integrated in the system that the change led to a reconstitution of the civilization with considerably different properties.

Civilizations change. Sometimes civilizations are closely integrated, sometimes loosely, and sometimes the integration becomes so faint and the external influences so considerable that we have difficulty determining whether they exist at all. Some civilizations never attain a high degree of integration and some remain at a well-integrated stage for a long time. Perfect integration is approached but never achieved. If it were, change would be impossible — a condition that is apparently attained in some primitive cultures, which are in what physicists call a "steady" state, involving a minimum of adjustment, as distinguished from the "stable state" of an artifact.

Civilizations are composed of a multitude of integrated "systems" — regional and provincial systems of government, agricultural and industrial districts — each of which is broken down

still further. I am taking this use of the term "system" from
Sorokin. Alternatively, using Kroeber's term (*Anthropology*,
p. 311), civilizations can be seen as being composed of "patterns"
— systems of art, philosophy, religion that are again broken
down into various schools and movements. The patterns are
the arrangements that give the parts a relationship to one another and to the civilization as a whole, whereas systems have
their own unity, regardless of whether they happen to form a
part of a still larger system. The sub-systems are like blocks
that a child uses to build a castle. The patterns are like strands
in a woven rug. Patterns are best studied in relation to the
system they compose; we should study Impressionist art with reference to the society in which it existed, although we can study
Russian government to see how it functions without concerning
ourselves with Russian history.

NOTE

Some Terms

Anthropologists use the term "society" to refer to groups of people and
the term "cultural" to refer to the way these people think, feel, and behave.
Thus it has become proper to use the term "society" to refer only to the
general category, because as soon as you refer to any specific society, you
are talking about the culture. Historians, on the other hand, prefer to talk
about "societies" and reserve "culture" for their aesthetic and philosophical
aspects. I lean toward the anthropologist's viewpoint in this book, but
with feelings of guilt and occasional inconsistencies.

Coulborn prefers to substitute the term "civilized society" for "civilization" since the latter has too many connotations and because civilized people
can be clearly discerned where the outline of a civilization may be obliterated
(*Journal of World History*, Vol. VIII, Number 1 (1964), 18). I sympathize,
but the term "society" is equally ambiguous. We shall have to endure
terms with multiple meanings.

4: THE UNIQUE CHARACTER
OF EACH CIVILIZATION

Marco Polo was struck by the fact that the Chinese ate differently, thought differently, and had different customs from the Europeans. The patterns of their activities and ideas gave distinctive qualities to their respective cultures. Since the patterns relate to one another in a culture, it is usually possible to distinguish the outstanding characteristics of various peoples.

Concentration on the outstanding differences between Englishmen and Americans enables the social historian to characterize each country. Concentration on their similarities enables him to characterize their common culture, and thereby to distinguish the civilization to which they belong from other civilizations. To an American the differences might be important: the Englishmen might seem old-fashioned, remote, charming. To the Chinese, the similarities might be overriding: the Westerners seem technologically-oriented, dynamic, superficial. Individual cultures and whole civilizations thus can be characterized in a few terms or a single word.

Though we may characterize civilizations as a whole, we can best see the characteristics operating by comparing individuals, preferably individuals who are operating under identical conditions. For example, if you give a volleyball to a group of Western soldiers stationed in Korea, they will form two teams and play a competitive game. If you give the same ball in the same area to Korean soldiers, they will form a circle and kick the ball to one another. The Westerners keep score, play aggressively, achieve recognition by blending their abilities with those of teammates, and discuss the game after it is played. The Koreans keep no score, yield readily to other participants, achieve recognition by adroit individual manipulation, and talk little about the game after it is over. The way in which the individuals behave, and the form their recreation takes, reflects their society.

But at the same time, their culture is what it is because they do these things: the form of their game fits the individuals and the individuals fit the form: each modifies the other. The Westerners say it is "like the Koreans" to play in the manner they do. What they mean is that the Koreans' approach to recreation seems consistent with the approach to other things they do, that they have characteristic ways of behavior.

All the characteristics of a civilization, then, tend to relate to and modify one another. Nations tend to borrow from one another, developments in art and history in one area tend to be modified by those in other areas, and all these interacting and modifying elements tend to give an image to the civilization as a whole. This image, in turn, pervades the civilization and tends to influence and modify the disparate elements. Once these characteristics become established, they tend to persist through this reciprocal reinforcement, even though the civilization is undergoing momentous change. Thus Spengler and Toynbee take it for granted that the civilization of Homer is the civilization of Diocletian.

Spengler sees this image as a "soul" that appears at the beginning of a civilization's existence and pervades and directs it throughout. This view has been modified by Kroeber who sees the "soul" only as a generalization about the relatedness of the patterns to the whole (Spengler, *Decline of the West,* I: pp. 179-180; Kroeber, *Style and Civilizations,* pp. 101-102). Though I concur with Kroeber's modifications, Spengler certainly has conveyed the early appearance of the image in saying that the soul exists at the "birth" of the civilization: we can't be sure a civilization is there until we can discern an image.

Spengler has also been criticized for overdrawing his characterizations and for overstressing their pervasiveness. For him, "pure and limitless space" describes the West, "the sensuously-present individual body" the Greco-Roman, a "wandering way" the Chinese, and so on (*Decline of the West,* I: pp. 183,190). But I find these sharply drawn contrasts useful. We all know they are simplifications and that they may have to be modified for different situations, but if civilizations are going to be described at all, we must try to pick out those characteristics that make them unique. A watered-down, excessively elaborated description is difficult to work with. Somerset Maugham has pointed out that if a novelist is too detailed and exact in his characterization, his character appears senseless and inconsistent. We are no longer able to apprehend his image.

Inevitably characterization is a matter of individual judgment and inevitably it will reflect the personality of that individual. But this is also true, of course, of the writing of any narrative history: when data is plentiful, the observer must select; when it is lacking, he must draw inferences. The danger in characterization is that once it has been made it tends to commit the observer in further observations he may make. If he says that Western civilization is Faustian — i.e. that its representatives tend to have an indomitable urge to explore, penetrate or meddle — he may feel he ought to apologize for individuals who do not fit this characterization, or he may seek further evidence to prove that after all, despite appearances, they do fit. But this is a problem inherent in all hypothetical formulations. Characterizers, model builders, and image-makers must expect their creations to be modified or even destroyed by empirical data.

Notes

a.   The Universal Volleyball

The Egyptian pyramid, the Babylonian ziggurat, and the Christian crypt may all have their prototypes in the mountain cave (Lewis Mumford, *The City in History*, p. 9). Most cultures will have some form of sculpture unless, as in Islam, it is excluded by a strong culture pattern.

On the other hand, some aspects of societies may be similar wherever they appear. This is true, for instance, of irrigation, which requires a particular set of conditions in order to be effective. Therefore, though it may have been invented several times in varying cultures, irrigation is carried on everywhere by almost identical techniques (Victor Von Hagen, *The Realm of the Incas*, p. 72).

b.   The Image

The concept of the image as a shared and constantly modified picture of a system comes from Kenneth Boulding's *The Image*. Images of civilizations have been discerned by other comparative historians under other names such as a "formative principle" (Danilevsky), a "common consciousness" (Dawson), a "central meaning" (Sorokin), a "controlling ideology" (Clough), or a "Weltanschauung" (Schweitzer).

WINGATE COLLEGE LIBRARY
WINGATE, N. C.

c. The Depth of Characterization

Quigley says the culture described by Spengler and Toynbee and most Greco-Roman historians reached only superficial levels in classical society. This is true of all civilizations and all history in that the "high" culture has always been made by a minority. And yet, a Russian peasant is different from a French peasant. Peasants may have common characteristics in that there are limitations in the possible ways they can do their work, but all the same, they tend to differentiate themselves and the differentiation probably can be accounted for more by the nature of the cultures they share than by the nature of the land they till.

5: BOUNDARIES OF CIVILIZATIONS

If civilizations have an internal consistency, if they have discernible, unique characteristics, then they can be distinguished from one another. Not that they don't interact and collide and occasionally destroy one another. But once they have a chance to develop, once they become sufficiently large and complex, they can withstand a considerable amount of buffeting and still retain their identity. One civilization rarely receives material from another without changing the nature of that material to fit its own patterns. Anything that can be transmitted without change is concerned with basic, mechanistic functions — and if such things are not transmitted they may be reinvented anyway when the need arises.

A good measure of agreement has already been reached on the methods for delineating civilizations, and on when and where these civilizations existed. Disagreements exist on whether more stress should be placed on the existence of specific patterns such as language, religion, technological development and forms of art, or on the existence of historical processes and distinctive phases of development. Disagreements also persist on the margins of time and space, on whether smaller, less developed, or interrupted cultures should be called civilizations at all, and whether long, irregular periods of history should be studied as one or more civilizations. Out of this discussion separate civilizations are generally distinguished in the following areas:

the Far East between 2000 B.C. and the present
India between 2500 B.C. and the present
Egypt between 4000 B.C. and 300 B.C.
the Middle East between 4000 B.C. and the present
the Mediterranean between 3000 B.C. and 1500 A.D.
Western Europe between 700 A.D. and the present
Central America between 1 A.D. and 1600 A.D.
western South America between 1 A.D. and 1600 A.D.

Further, there is a pronounced but less frequent tendency to distinguish an Islamic civilization around the Southern Mediterranean between 500 and the present, an Orthodox civilization in eastern Europe at roughly the same period and a civilization in Japan, since possibly 400 B.C., that has been sufficiently distinct from China to merit separate classification.

The delineation of civilizations is usually unsatisfactory, often esoteric and sometimes rather quibbly, but it is important because in any attempt to portray the history of a civilization it is necessary to understand the reasons for its limits and divisions; because a measure of agreement on civilizations by the comparative historians will make their own writing more useful for comparison with one another; and because generalizations about recurrence will have more meaning when the structures of the civilizations in which recurrences take place are better understood.

The relationship between historical recurrences and civilizations is particularly important. If we are interested in Napoleon, we might explain his failure to unify Europe in terms of his own shortcomings, or in terms of a peculiar recuperative vitality manifested in Europe. But was it the man or the situation that prevented unification? Or was it a fortuitous combination of both? We begin to look for other examples in history. Alexander also failed to create a long-standing empire. Was this because he and Napoleon faced similar situations? And how was it that these two most famous and gifted men failed to do what an Augustus, a Chandragupta, or an Ivan III did succeed in doing? If we study the careers of these men we can come up with some answers that probably will throw more light on the career of Napoleon. But we shall have a deeper understanding still if we also try to understand the context of the civilization in which the empire builders lived, if we can discern whether they were, to use one of Toynbee's more preposterous phrases, "philosophically contemporaneous."

In discussing the delineation of civilizations, there is a tendency to be apologetic because there are so few examples. Toynbee is sorry because he can find only thirty while the lucky entomologist has all those millions of specimens to work on. He asks us to be patient because in a few hundred thousand years, if all goes well, which (he says) it probably won't, we shall have many more samples. More anthropologically-oriented historians, on the other hand, think we can partly make up for this difficulty by making studies of intermediate and primitive cultures, which will be easier to handle and will throw more light on methods of study in tackling the larger systems (Kroeber, *Style and Civilizations,* pp. 158-159; Christopher Dawson, *The Dynamics of World History*, p. 425) .

This is all very well when you are making suggestions for other people to carry out, but when you are thinking of tackling these problems yourself, it becomes frightening. Toynbee's maximum of thirty civilizations, or even the assessments of Spengler, Kroeber, Coulborn and Quigley at between eight and fifteen major civilizations, are already enough to occupy anyone for a lifetime. Anyone now living was born none too soon. As for the minor and derivative and humble cultures, they will be useful in time for criticism and verification. But, understandably, comparative historians have been gravitating toward Spengler's intuitive generalizations rather than Toynbee's perhaps more sophisticated delineations. There are not too few civilizations, there are too many — for any one man. So let the pioneers draw their material from an insufficient sample, as Spengler and Toynbee have done, and let these hypotheses be modified or destroyed by the detailed work of scholars, by reconsideration and by time.

NOTES

a. Spengler's Impenetrable Civilizations

We are inclined to be patronizing about Spengler on this subject of the mutual impenetrability of civilizations. Kroeber, fair and gentle writer that he is, tries to defend Spengler by pointing to the time in which he wrote and to the opposition he had to overcome. In so doing, Kroeber portrays Spengler as a pioneer, as a man who eloquently pointed the way. But I am by no means sure that Kroeber, and particularly his successors, have been any more helpful on this subject than Spengler. When the explanations are in, when we have mulled it over, civilizations are exclusive and impenetrable. Well, that's what Spengler said. Only he said it better.

b. On Distinguishing Successive Civilizations

Kroeber suggests the following criteria: "permanent conquest; establish-ment of a new religion, as rightly emphasized by Toynbee; expansion and retraction of area covered; severity of political, economic, aesthetic-ideo-logical breakdown between two cultures" (*Style and Civilization*, p. 145) . Toynbee did seem a bit bolder (or more reckless, depending on your viewpoint) about distinguishing successive civilizations in the same area, as in India and China, or in finding more than one in adjacent or overlapping areas, as in the Afro-Asian borderlands. But in his *Reconsiderations* he has retreated from these separations.

c. Civilizations vs. Primitive Cultures

How sharply civilizations should be distinguished from primitive cultures is still a subject of debate. To some writers, like Christopher Dawson and Lewis Mumford, primitive cultures seem to behave very like civilizations; to others, like Spengler and Coulborn, civilized behavior seems sharply distinguishable; still others, like Kroeber and Philip Bagby, have distinguished secondary cultures both from civilizations and from primitive cultures. Toynbee is inclined to count these less developed and interrupted cultures as civilizations. That is why he distinguished some twenty or thirty, as compared to about ten for most of the other comparative historians.

The extent of consensus thus far attained might be gauged by comparing the delineations of six comparative historians who have been most explicit on the subject (see Figure 1).

In compiling this chart I have taken the liberty of giving a date (preceded by 'c.') where the writer has indicated perhaps no more than a millennium. A question mark following a date indicates that the date is inferred. A question mark without a date indicates that no inference was attempted.

Most of this material is taken from the charts between the volumes of Spengler's *Decline*; table V in the Somervell abridgement of Toynbee's *Study*, preceding I: 567 (with a few modifications from *Reconsiderations*); Kroeber's *Configurations*, pp. 663-758; Bagby's *Culture and History*, pp. 165-170; Coulborn's *The Origin of Civilized Societies*, pp. 3-9; and Quigley's *Evolution of Civilizations*, pp. 37 and 93.

Coulborn's datings in primary civilizations are invariably earlier than those of the others, probably because he is trying to indicate where "civilization" has its origins rather than determine whether "civilizations" could be said to exist. Toynbee, Kroeber, Bagby and Quigley would agree, I imagine, that high-level cultures existed in these periods, but they would either deny that they had attained the level of civilization, or, more likely, contend that the classification of these periods is still uncertain.

Some comments on the individual areas may be helpful in decoding the chart:

The Far East — Toynbee dates the Sinic civilization from 1500 B.C. to 172 A.D. and the Far Eastern civilization from 500 to 1853 A.D. Quigley makes a similar division for his two civilizations: the Sinic from 2000 B.C. to 400 A.D., and the Chinese from 400 to 1930 A.D.

Toynbee thinks the separation of modern Chinese civilization is open to question (*Study*, XII: 173-183). He and probably some of the others would agree with Coulborn that a high level

Area of Origin	SPENGLER	TOYNBEE	KROEBER	BAGBY	COULBORN	QUIGLEY
FAR EAST	Chinese 1300 B.C.-220 A.D.	Sinic/ Far Eastern 1500 B.C.-1853 A.D. "Far Eastern Offshoot" 500-1853 A.D.	Chinese 1200 B.C.-1400 A.D. Japanese 400 B.C.-1800 A.D.	Chinese 1500 B.C.-present	Chinese c. 2800 B.C.-present	Sinic/ Chinese 2000 B.C.-1930 A.D. Japanese 100 B.C.-1950 A.D.
INDIA	Indian 1500-200 (?) B.C.	Indic 1500 B.C.-475 A.D.	Indian 600 B.C.-1200 A.D.	Indian 1500 B.C.-present	Indian c. 2500 B.C.-present	Hindu 1500 B.C.-1900 A.D.
MIDDLE EAST	Babylonian 3000-200 (?) B.C. Magian 1 A.D.-present	Sumero-Akkadian c. 3500 B.C.-100 A.D. Islamic 1300 A.D.-present	Islam 530-1500 A.D.	Babylonian c. 300-100 B.C. Near Eastern 1 A.D.-present	Mesopotamian c. 4500-600 (?) B.C. Islamic 500 (?) A.D.-present	Mesopotamian c. 6000-300 B.C. Islamic 600-1940 A.D.
EGYPT	Egyptian 2900-1205 B.C.	Egyptaic c. 4000-1175 B.C.	Egyptian c. 3315-663 B.C.	Egyptian c. 2700-500 B.C.	Egyptian c. 4500-600 (?) B.C.	Egyptian c. 5500-300 B.C.
MEDITERRANEAN		Minoan c. 3000-1400 B.C.			Cretan c. 3000-1100 (?) B.C.	Cretan 3000-1100 B.C.
EASTERN EUROPE	Classical 1100 B.C.-200 A.D.	Hellenic 1100 B.C.-378 A.D. Orthodox 700-1768 A.D.	Mediterranean 1200 B.C.-1453 A.D	Classical 1200 B.C.-300 A.D.	Graeco-Roman 1200 (?) B.C.-500 (?) A.D. Byzantine 600 (?) A.D.-present	Classical 1100 B.C.-500 A.D. Orthodox 600 A.D.-present
WESTERN EUROPE	Western 900-2200 A.D.	Western 700 A.D.-present	Occidental 800 A.D.-present	Western European 900 A.D.-present	Western 500 (?) A.D.-present	Western 500 A.D.-present
CENTRAL AMERICA	Mexican 160 B.C.-1521 A.D.	Middle American 500 B.C.-1821 A.D.	Meso-American ? - 1550 (?) A.D.	Middle American 1-1550 A.D.	Middle American c. 1800 B.C.-1600 (?) A.D.	Meso-American 1000 B.C.-1550 A.D.
SOUTH AMERICA	Andean 500 (?) B.C.-1533 A.D.	Andean 500 (?) B.C.-1533 A.D.	Andean ? - 1550 (?) A.D.	Peruvian 1-1550 A.D.	Andean 1000 B.C.-1533 A.D.	Andean

Figure 1

of culture existed in China before 1500 B.C., but the question seems to be whether this culture should be classified as a civilization. Spengler rejects the separate classification of Japan (*Decline*, II: 49); Bagby thinks the classification is still open to question; Coulborn apparently includes it with the Chinese.

India — Toynbee adds a second civilization, the Hindu (800 A.D. to the present), but he also grants this is debatable. The disagreement on whether there was an Indian civilization as far back as the third and fourth millenium is similar to the disagreement on the dating of the Chinese.

The Middle East — this seems to be the most difficult area to classify. Kroeber apparently would have included an "Ancient Near Eastern Civilization" in an unfinished "roster" published after his death (*A Roster of Civilizations and Culture*, p. 21). This would probably have corresponded to the Mesopotamian-Sumerian-Babylonian civilization distinguished by others. Toynbee's Sumero-Akkadian civilization represents a revised view developed in *Reconsiderations*. Toynbee and Quigley distinguish a separate Hittite civilization in the second millenium B.C. Kroeber and Coulborn consider the Jews to have had a separate civilization beginning in the second millenium B.C., while Quigley includes the Jews, Phoenicians and Carthaginians in a Caananite civilization (2200-100 B.C.). Kroeber and Coulborn distinguish an Iranian civilization beginning in the first millenium B.C. Toynbee discerns a Syriac civilization that seems to have specialized in hatching religions (1100 B.C.-969 A.D.).

Egypt — Considerable agreement here. No one seems to have accepted Petrie's view that successive civilizations existed in Egypt.

Mediterranean — recent research on Crete indicates that there were Mycenaean influences both on Crete and on Greece. At present, however, the culture of Crete seems to be considered as distinct from that of Greece. Spengler regards the civilization of Crete as an Egyptian offshoot, a view unsupported by later scholars. Bagby considers it a "secondary" culture, not a civilization. Agreement on Classical civilization is fairly close, though Kroeber includes the Byzantine civilization with the Roman.

Eastern Europe — Spengler, Kroeber and Bagby incorporate Byzantium in their Magian, Mediterranean and Near Eastern civilizations respectively. Russia gets mixed reviews. It is treated as a separate civilization by Spengler and Toynbee, as part of Byzantine civilization by Coulborn and Quigley, as European by Kroeber and as uncertain by Bagby. Coulborn's last position was to regard the Byzantine as a separate civilization.

Western Europe — the only disagreement here is on whether to include the Dark Ages or to start Western civilization at some point where recovery has begun.

America — originally Toynbee distinguished three civilizations in Central America. He reduced them to one in his *Reconsiderations* (*Study,* XII: 173-183). According to Coulborn, Kroeber apparently concluded, after the publication of *Configurations,* that there was enough evidence to warrant delineation of civilizations in Central and South America. In his revision of *Anthropology* (1948) he still refers to Meso-American and Andean "high cultures" (pp. 777-801). Spengler never elaborates on Peruvian civilization. He couples it once with the Mexican (*Decline,* II: 46), but he never classifies it.

SOURCES

A. COMPARATIVE HISTORY IN GENERAL

An evaluation of the major books is given in the bibliography.

B. THE CONCEPT OF CIVILIZATIONS

Oswald Spengler, *The Decline of the West,* I: 103-113, the idea of culture; Arnold Toynbee, *A Study of History,* I: 17-51, "The Field of Historical Study"; A. L. Kroeber, *Anthropology,* pp. 252-265, "The Nature of Culture"; Pitirim A. Sorokin, *Social Philosophies of an Age of Crisis,* pp. 275-279, "The Civilizational or Cultural Supersystems"; Philip Bagby, *Culture and History,* pp. 159-182, "Civilizations"; Rushton Coulborn, *The Origin of Civilized Societies,* pp. 16-21, distinguishing factors in a civilized society; Carroll Quigley, *The Evolution of Civilizations,* Ch. 3, "Groups, Societies, Civilizations."

The civilization concept, as seen by Spengler, Toynbee and Kroeber, is attacked by Sorokin, *Social Philosophies,* pp. 205-209. But Kroeber shows that Sorokin's concept of cultural fluctuations correlates rather closely with the delineations of others (*Style and Civilizations,* pp. 179-181).

C. THE REALITY OF CIVILIZATIONS

Sorokin, *Social Philosophies of an Age of Crisis,* pp. 205-8, "Are Civilizations Cultural Congeries or Unified Systems?"; Kroeber, *A Roster of Civilizations,* pp. 10-11; Kroeber, *Style and Civilizations,* pp. 173-182, "Sorokin"; Kroeber, *The Nature of Culture,* p. 4, the danger of reification; Bagby answers in *American Anthropologist,* Vol. LV: pp. 535-554, "Culture and the Causes of Culture"; the suggestion that civilizations are only "matters of convenience" is put forth forcefully by Pieter Geyl, *Debates with Historians,* pp. 133-4 and R. G. Collingwood, *The Idea of History,* pp. 163-5.

D. THE INTEGRATION OF CIVILIZATIONS

Sorokin, *Social and Cultural Dynamics,* abridged ed., pp. 2-17, "Problems of Cultural Integration."

E. THE CHARACTERIZATION OF CIVILIZATIONS

Spengler, *Decline,* I: 183-216, "Apollinian, Faustian and Magian Soul"; Sorokin, *Social and Cultural Dynamics,* abridged ed., pp. 20-39, four systems of culture, and *Social Philosophies,* pp. 277-8, the concept of the "major premise"; Kroeber, *Style and Civilizations,* pp. 99-103, reflections on Spengler's characterizations; Christopher Dawson, *The Dynamics of World History,* pp. 41-3, 56-9, the spiritual influence underlying a civilization; Bagby, *Culture and History,* pp. 117-121, evaluation of characterization; Coulborn, *The Origin of Civilized Societies,* pp. 21-4, style as a mark of individuality; Quigley, *Evolution of Civilizations,* pp. 173-5, depth and breadth of characterization. Toynbee acknowledges that characterizations open "an interesting line of inquiry" (*Study,* III: 383), but he doesn't seem to inquire any further himself.

F. THE DELINEATIONS OF CIVILIZATIONS

Sources are included in Section Six, in the chart and its annotations. One other set of delineations should be mentioned: those of Flinders Petrie, in *The Revolutions of Civilisation,* pp. 11-74.

II

HOW CIVILIZATIONS DEVELOP

1: CHANGE AND CONTINUITY

Although civilizations change continuously, they maintain their identity for centuries. The change comes about because the civilization is a going, functioning system. When the actions of men break restraining customs and set off processes of development in part of the system, this in turn sets off related development in other parts of the system.

Despite change, civilizations maintain their identity once well-integrated patterns have been established. If changes are to be induced, they must have some relationship to these patterns, and leaders who fail to take these patterns into consideration are likely to be replaced.

It seems natural in describing these processes to fall back on organic terms: to talk about the growth or unfolding of a civilization on one hand and about its exhaustion and death on the other. This gives pain to many students of society who feel that after all, Spengler not withstanding, cultures are not organisms (*The Decline of the West,* I: 104). These terms arise, however, not only because no better ones are available but also because the analogies are so tempting. Men, like cultures, change constantly yet maintain their identity. Yet many do seem to maintain only a steady state, to go on living without becoming. If they do develop, it is because something inside them drives them to it, or because qualities they have are allowed to develop by the culture in which they live. Once a man's patterns become established, it is difficult for him or anyone else to change them. Eventually a man runs down, disintegrates, dies, or is overwhelmed by external circumstances or killed by accident or design.

Civilizations are living systems; men are living systems too.

Notes

a. The Internal Motif

The emphasis on immanent or internal change is especially strong in the writings of Spengler, Toynbee and Sorokin. This approach has been fruitful in that it has led us to look more closely at systems themselves in trying to ascertain causes of revolution, urbanization or population decline. But the approach has served its purpose, and it is well that less deterministic writers like Kroeber, Dawson and Quigley are willing to accept the possibility that internal changes might be greatly modified by random external factors.

b. Disintegration vs. Social Order

The tension between the tendency toward disintegration and the drive for social order is described by Kenneth Boulding (*The Image*, p. 19). Spengler (*Decline*, II: 172), Toynbee (*Study*, I: 191-192; III: 245-249) and Shepard Clough (*The Rise and Fall of Civilization*, p. 207) are in agreement that whatever the underlying impersonal forces, it is the action of men, usually a few dynamic individuals, that creates new levels of social order. (See also Dawson, *The Dynamics of World History*, pp. 57-58).

c. Social Organisms

It might be worth noting, in passing, that students of the biological sciences sometimes classify families and societies as organisms. To Paul Weisz (*The Science of Biology*, pp. 111-114) anything is alive that maintains and reproduces itself. Societies fall into this category, and the men in them are no more autonomous nor less specialized than cells that compose a body. And you may say of cultures, as Weisz does of living organisms, that they may be "envisaged as transient constructions built out of materials 'borrowed' temporarily from the environment" (*The Science of Biology*, p. 306).

All the tangible traits of a culture are wrung from the physical environment by the labor of man. And all ideas are generalizations about these tangible traits, other men, or the environment itself.

2: ORIGINS AND LIBERATION

Often the characteristics of a civilization becomes manifest rather rapidly, so that Spengler could speak of the birth of its soul. The appearance of Gothic cathedrals in the eleventh century dramatically commemorates the birth of Faustian Man. What really has happened, of course, is that we have identified a civilization through certain characteristics, we trace these characteristics back as far as we can, and the earliest point at which we think they emerge we call the beginning a civilization. When the civilization has begun to develop, it may continue to exist long after the cultures from which it originally sprang have lost their identity through merger, division, disintegration, or destruction. Thus the Jewish civilization survived the Mesopotamian, the Byzantine survived the Classical.

The confluence of patterns that had to do with the origins of the first civilizations may have been related to environmental challenges, but there is still considerable uncertainty about the nature of these challenges, and disagreement about whether civilizations were invented more than once. But there must have been some compelling reason for man to change his way of life, moving from a nomadic existence based primarily on hunting to a sedentary agricultural life in the great river valleys of the world (Rushton Coulborn, *The Origin of Civilized Societies,* pp. 67-109, modified in "Structure and Process in the Rise and Fall of Civilized Societies," p. 410). The challenge involved in this transition must have been immensely difficult, requiring astonishing changes in political and economic concepts, and probably producing many failures before two civilizations — the Sumerian and the Egyptian — emerged nearly at the same time. Toynbee suggests a possible human challenge: the migration of peoples (which might have an environmental origin) often forces another people to move and face the challenge of a new situation, or else produces an intermixture of peoples that sometimes precedes the flowering of a new civilization (*A Study of History*, abridged ed., I: 75-79; also Christopher Dawson, *The Dynamics of World History*, p. 8).

In view of the importance of understanding the nature of patterns, you might suppose that there would be a great deal of concern about the origins or causes of civilizations. This has not been the case. There has been a tendency to avoid the study of origins that derives, I suspect, from the comparative historians' rejection of the narrative historians' cause-and-effect approach to history. The historians of that period tended to look for the cause of World War I in the sequence of diplomatic events in the years preceding, without giving sufficient consideration to the social atmosphere of the entire civilization. The implication of looking for cause in preceding events was that ultimate cause was to be found in whatever came first — the origin of the situation — rather than in overall relationships. But more recently, as narrative historians have responded more to relational and less to sequential cause, comparative historians like Coulborn and Quigley seem to have been able to pursue the study of origins without apology.

It is clear that the understanding of a particular aspect of a culture is bound up with the understanding of the culture itself. And if we can see it in its formative phase, we can distinguish better the patterns that are inclined to become more elaborated and more obscured in later phases. Moreover, if you are studying parallel developments in different cultures, anomalies may sometimes be explained not in the contemporary events, but in pattern variations that derive from formative periods. Thus the Russian Revolution in many aspects followed paths analogous to earlier European revolutions. We should expect, therefore, to learn a good deal about the Russian Revolution by comparing it, as Crane Brinton has done, with the French and the English. But in many respects the society emerging from the Russian Revolution differed considerably from the France of the nineteenth century. These differences derive partly from the intervening development of the industrial revolution, but also partly from differences in the patterns of Russian and French history.

Some form of ritualized religion is repeatedly associated with the early stage of cultural development. Comparative historians agree almost unanimously upon its dominant role in the formation of cultures. This is as true of those who, like Coulborn and Spengler, regard religion purely as a factor to be considered in the study of societies, as it is of those who, like Toynbee and Dawson, regard religion as "the foundations on which the great civilizations rest." Some kind of theocratic leadership seems to be necessary to inspire the support of the members of a culture that is still too fragile to withstand internal disunity. Often this religious unity seems to be closely related to an economic system that places strong emphasis on the value of the land and on family relationships. Sometimes it is closely connected with government, as in the Iranian and Chinese civilizations; at others distinct, as in the Classical and Western.

And if religion forms the unifying element in most developing or reviving civilizations, the nature of that religion will surely influence the process of secularization that accompanies a civilization's development. Secularization — the gradual freeing of patterns from the dominance of the original ritualized religion — seems to be a recurrent and necessary process. This process, which may last many centuries, involves the freeing of all political, economic and aesthetic patterns from their close ties with religion. Without secularization, civilization cannot develop. Apparently no religious crystalization or synthesis can be maintained except at the cost of internal ossification, the smothering of all processes of development by an autocratic priesthood.

The study of origins, then, and particularly the study of religion will frequently have tremendous relevance to the understanding of secular problems developing in later phases. And comparisons of secular problems will frequently be clarified by comparisons of origins.

NOTES

a. The Agrarian Image

Boulding points out that an overwhelming transition of image was required in the "agricultural revolution." However did men bring themselves to plow up the green, fruitful land and replace it with apparently barren, brown soil?

b. The Diffusionist Theory vs. the Theory of Independent Origins

There is still some controversy about whether the breakthrough that led to the creation of civilizations occurred only once or several times independently. The appearance of individual civilizations in pockets thousands of miles apart suggests to me that civilizations were independently reinvented under similar environmental conditions.

And yet there is something unsatisfactory about this explanation. Jaspers wonders why, within two millenia, four civilizations should have formed in four separate river valleys (the Nile, the Tigris-Euphrates, the Indus and the Hwang-ho) and why two others much later under different conditions in America (*The Origin and Goal of History*, p. 13). And why after this last ice age and not after any other ice age? Had man come along that much biologically? There are still pieces missing from the puzzle. The answer may involve areas we have not probed, cultural extrasensory perception or something like that.

My emotional preference for the independent origins is further undercut by two widely acclaimed recent publications, both of which take it for granted that civilization was invented only once, in Mesopotamia (Lewis Mumford, *The City in History*, pp. 90-92; William McNeill, *The Rise of The West*, Chapter III, "The Diffusion of Civilization"). But Coulborn, who gave more attention to the problem than Mumford or McNeill, was still maintaining in 1968 that the diffusionist theory is untenable.

3: Collapses and Recoveries

Once a civilization has achieved a measure of coherence, with an established relationship between its components, potentialities for change become increasingly limited. This applies to systems at all levels and to the patterns that compose them. The limits of a particular civilization depend largely but not entirely on the character it assumed in its formative period. Once established, the various patterns of a civilization tend to develop in relation to one another until each has achieved its potential.

For example, the development of geometry was the Greek style of mathematics, a pattern in their culture. It appears to be related to the Greek emphasis on proportion and their preference for visible and tangible bodies — hence the preference for integral numbers and the avoidance of negative numbers and fractions. It is easy to see that once the full possibilities of geometry are reached, creativity in the field must die out, or mathematical activity must shift to some other form, or some way must be found to add new elements to geometry that will give scope for further development. If such additions and changes were made, however, the resulting configurations might bear very little relation to what had been called geometry. They would come to be classified under a new name and to be thought of as components of a different kind of mathematics.

But if geometry develops in an integrated society, if it is one manifestation of a Greco-Roman preference for tangibly present forms, related to the nude statue, the "sensuous cult of the Olympian gods," and the politically individual city states (Spengler, *Decline*, I: 183), it is likely to change only if the whole culture is likewise in a process of transition. Otherwise, if new elements were added, geometry would lose its relationship to its culture. Such changes do take place, but rarely unless the culture as a whole is on the threshhold of disintegration. In the case of the Greeks, the changes did not take place. "What they would do with their geometrical and whole-number

manner of style, they achieved. Other mathematical possibilities . . . were simply left to be realized by other peoples and
other times. . . . " (Kroeber, *Anthropology*, p. 330) .

The geometry pattern, then, is inherently limited. Clearly all
patterns tend to reach culminations unless new material is
gradually and constantly added. And when the limits of possibilities are sensed, there is likely to be some casting around.
After a vein or complex of veins has been developed, miners
face a dilemma. They can explore subordinate, low-yield areas
further; they can go back and try to find some ore overlooked
when the major veins were freely yielding; they can look for
new veins; they can close the mine and dig another; they can
give up.

Art patterns are somewhat similar to the patterns of a mine.
After an idea or major complex of ideas has been developed
and explored, the developing artist is faced with a dilemma.
Whereas fifty years previously artists were creating freely and
prolifically, now they find that the additions they can make to
the existing pattern are of a secondary or elaborative nature.
Some will content themselves with doing this, some will repeat
the patterns of immediate predecessors, some will return to
earlier periods hoping that when development came, some possibilities were overlooked. Some will cast about, will feel
uncomfortable, will experiment, will challenge the old patterns
instead of trying to develop them further. Some will give up.

Individual culminations of patterns, occurring in succession,
form a culmination for the civilization as a whole. The culmination tends to come rather early in the life of the pattern, long
before the creative phase has completely ended. Manifestations
of creativeness appear long after the underlying factors that give
rise to them have begun to change. In China, for instance, the
Hundred Schools of philosophy (c. 500-300 B.C.) had given
form to the civilization's outlook before the first of a series of
great empires was formed. Sculpture had two important periods
of development during the Han (200 B.C.-100 A.D.) and T'ang
(600-500 A.D.) Empires, poetry reaching a long high active
period (200-800 A.D.) through the time of the Three Kingdoms
and the T'ang, painting reaching a peak during the period of
the Sung (950-1100 A.D.) . Though there is development in
drama and the novel in post-Sung periods, they seem less dynamic

than the earlier periods. By the time of the highly refined Sung period, decline was setting in, but as early as the Three Kingdoms period most of the patterns had been set, and the philosophical patterns, which proved to be central to Chinese style, had been clearly delineated nearly a millennium before general decline had set in.

Once a pattern or series of related patterns have passed a culmination, three possibilities remain open: they may disintegrate and disappear, they may become fixed in a steady state, or they may experience a period of transition in which disintegration takes place while new material is being added, before the onset of further development. Civilizations, like lesser systems, face these alternatives: they either disintegrate, ossify, or reconstitute themselves and develop further.

In all systems, in all patterns, there are forces working both for integration and for disintegration. In earlier periods of development, the former dominate until the culminating point of a given pattern or system. If the subsequent disintegration continues unchecked in a civilization for a long period, the civilization may cease to exist. It dies. Between 100 and 700 A.D. the Roman Empire virtually disappeared from the Western Mediterranean. The culture in this area changed so rapidly that hardly anyone would find in it a unity and continuity of existence. The lesser patterns that compose a civilization of course disintegrate and disappear frequently, even when its total processes may tend toward integration and unity.

It may happen that the process of integration is checked through the ossification of the most significant patterns. A strong central government, by maintaining the system as it is without permitting normal changes, may enable the civilization to hold the line for a very long time. But it will be sterile, its forms endlessly repeated, its creativity dried up, its activities without meaning beyond mere survival. This appears to have happened to the Egyptian civilization and more recently in the Chinese and Islamic civilizations. In a civilization capable of strong centralized control of political and economic functions, it can happen again. Ossification occurs far more commonly within the subsystems of a civilization. These often become so overelaborated that they are no longer able to function, but they may continue to exist in a ceremonial capacity while their functions are taken over by other systems that have relevance to a particular problem. The changes in the relationships between the British monarchy and parliament, or between the Japanese emperor and shogunate, will serve as examples.

The process of disintegration may be resolved by internal effort, or by the impingement from outside of new material and new attitudes, probably resulting in the violent collapse of the old, unadapted framework. But then, because new answers are being sought, or because the internal disruption makes possible the absorption of alien ideas and artifacts, a new period of development may take place. What appeared to be a disastrous disintegration of old patterns turns out to be the creation of a condition from which a new and perhaps greater development can take place. The collapse and recovery of the T'ang empire and the emergence of the western Renaissance are examples of reconstitutions of this kind. If men had adhered to cherished Confucian or Christian patterns, their respective civilizations might have disappeared. As it was, they were able to make a transition to unfamiliar patterns, the pattern of Chinese empire was given a viable foundation, the Renaissance took place and the modern phase of Western history became one of fresh development.

This concept of reconstitution raises hob with those of us who are trying to arrange history in an orderly manner. If disintegrating civilizations can recover and go on to further phases of development, it is obviously going to be very difficult to cut them into orderly segments, with this phase lasting 312 years and that phase 435 years. It is going to be difficult to make accurate predictions about the doom of those still in existence. Revelation can do that just about as accurately and far more impressively. To make matters worse, the frequent intrusion of alien civilizations in these periods makes it difficult to decide whether recovery has taken place or whether the disintegrating civilization has simply been replaced by another. Is the Babylonian civilization a separate entity or a second phase of Sumerian civilization? To describe the fall of the Roman Empire must you, as Gibbon did, tell the story of Byzantium as well?

What does emerge from this concept, though, is a striking similarity between formative periods and periods of disintegration. In both, things are in flux, and while men have great opportunities to share their destinies, they also face great risk of failure. And men pay for the glories, achievements and security of periods of integration with the loss of their capacity to do much more than manage a going concern. They can achieve great things within the system, but they can not change the system. So you can say that there are periods of high integration and periods of low integration. In the latter there are both disintegrating and formative forces in action, and only in retrospect can you be certain which proved dominant.

After all these modifications, how much is it possible to generalize about the formation and development of civilizations? Perhaps a symphonic analogy would be useful: the theme or themes of a symphony are roughly equivalent to the central idea or the symbols by which we characterize civilizations. The completion of the exposition is equivalent to the culmination of a civilization. The development is equivalent to disintegration, in which the original compact material is exploited, considered, elaborated, but little new is added. The recapitulation may be compared to those aspects of development that have to do with the re-examination of earlier times, the seeking for the restoration of basic foundations. The coda might represent the final collapse, the end, or it might prove to be a codetta leading to new themes, enabling new combinations and development to take place, the equivalent of reconstitution. If you were listening to a familiar symphony you would know what the coda signified, but if you were hearing it for the first time, you would have to wait and see. Should the development be carried too far, without recapitulation or coda, the thematic material becoming more worn out and repetitive, the symphony, like some civilizations, would become ossified, losing its interest. If the terminating coda is followed after a pause by a new movement beginning new themes in a new time and key, this is the equivalent of a heroic age (see p. 115) in an affiliated civilization, the formation of a new set of patterns.

Civilizations, like symphonies, retain characteristic patterns notwithstanding fluxes of formation, disintegration and reconstitution.

Notes

a. Alternative Conceptions of Culmination

Toynbee's conception of the breakdown of a civilization in another sense also describes the culminations of the patterns of a civilization. He sees a breakdown as a retrospective selection from what proved a crucial turning-point in the civilization's history, the most significant in a series of culminations.

A number of comparative historians, including Spengler, Christopher Dawson and Lewis Mumford, see the culmination as arising from a basic departure from the traditional reinforcements of the formative culture: ritualistic religion, an agrarian economy and a tight-knit family system. This, as we shall see (Chapters III and IV), does describe the process in which the patterns of feudal society reach their culmination, but it does not necessarily mark the culmination of a civilization as a whole.

b. Disintegration: Good or Bad?

The term "disintegration" unavoidably carries negative connotations. It is true that to see a man or a house in the process of disintegration is an unpleasant experience, and no doubt living in a disintegrating culture can be unpleasant too. But a high degree of integration also involves unpleasantness, as many who live in villages or highly integrated suburbias have found out, whereas disintegration can be a necessary and liberating process.

c. The Ossification of Institutions

Toynbee sees ossification as the process that transforms institutions into "enormities." They become enormities when they continue to exist even though no longer able to meet the challenges for which they were constructed. Quigley regards this phenomenon as a normal tendency in the life of most systems: they are created to serve a purpose but gradually become so elaborated and encumbered with vested interests that their primary purpose becomes the maintaining of their own existence. Kenneth Bouding's concept of the image is also relevant here. He remarks that the most successful images are likely to persist as they were while the world moves on (*A Study of History*, IV: 133-245; *The Evolution of Civilizations*, Chapter 5; *The Image*, p. 79).

d. The Renaissance as a Reconstitution

The medieval/modern division of Western civilization, which most narrative historians accept, recognizes the existence of two relatively integrated periods that can be treated either separately or as a whole. The Renaissance is a period of disintegration and rebuilding that in retrospect appears to be a reconstruction of Western civilization. Thus medieval history is studied either as an entity in itself or as a period that will throw light on the reconstituted patterns of modern history.

e. Bowler's Continuum

Downing Bowler sees all forms, social and natural, as fluctuations on a continuum between pure energy and total complexity. Pure energy would be a condition in which there are no relationships between the entities of the system. Total complexity would be a condition in which all possible relationships between the entities had been fulfilled. The former represents complete disintegration, the latter the maximum possible degree of integration. Alternation between the poles of the continuum might be diagramed as follows:

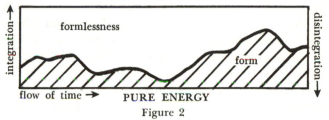

Figure 2

The peaks of these fluctuations would represent periods of relatively high integration.

4: REGULARITIES AND ANOMALIES

To speak of the behavior of civilizations in general is to imply that meaningful comparisons between them can be made. Obviously there are difficulties in generalizing about phenomena that differ tremendously in size, knowledge, technology and overall development. Our own civilization — all the more in the nuclear age — seems to have little relationship to Ancient Egypt or Sumeria. And yet, the resemblances are significant. All civilizations have been created as a by-product of human endeavor to solve basic problems of life. The problems differ somewhat, so do the solutions, but the common patterns are undeniable.

We learn by experience. Even ten experiences will teach us a great deal. If I see ten persons with a cold, I will observe certain reactions. Some of them will blow their noses in their handkerchiefs, some will use paper napkins, some might wipe them on their sleeves, some might let them run. None will roll down the stairs. None will stand on their heads in the bathtub. It is possible, therefore, to make some generalizations about reactions, even to make classifications. And I might even be able to make predictions about the eleventh person I meet who has a cold. The predictions might prove to be incorrect. But they probably will be closer to the mark than they would have been for the first of the unfortunates.

So I may expect a civilization suffering from an advanced case of total war to react in certain ways. It may continue to suffer or the conflict may be resolved. But I might expect the civilization to survive; I might even predict that it will not die. If it then does die, I can only say that it is an unusual case.

Recurrence is an obvious historical phenomenon. To insist that history is ever unique is simply to deny the obvious. But if these recurrences are considered without regard to their cultural context, they will be misread. The duplication of external form may mean nothing at all. The Renaissance revived Classical forms and the Victorian age revived Gothic forms, but we do not therefore bracket them together as revival periods.

On the other hand, externally different forms may serve the same purpose for different societies. Quigley argues, for instance, that Sumerian priests and Western knights performed similar functions as surplus accumulators. Spengler has given countless striking, if not convincing, examples of relations between, say, cathedrals, clocks and counterpoint. We may argue about the validity of some of these examples, but the point remains that phenomena appearing to have no relationship are seen in a new light when viewed in a comparative cultural context.

We need not go as far as Spengler in insisting that for every aspect of one civilization a corresponding aspect can be found in every other (*Decline,* I: 112). Recurrences are likely to be occasional, partial, or frequent, but rarely universal. Comparative historians are more likely to write about cultural "regularities." Certain phenomena, like feudal systems or portrait painting, appear regularly and seem to perform similar functions in most civilizations. But occasionally they do not appear or they are replaced by something else, which in that case is called an "anomaly." Ruth Benedict (see bibliography) conceives of a semicircular spectrum of possible behavior from which each culture selects a wedge. Each time certain kinds of behavior are selected, many other potential kinds are eliminated. Civilizations may take rather large slices of the cultural pie, but their chosen patterns still leave extensive blank areas. A civilization that has an aesthetic bent may not develop a philosophy of depth. Even forms that seem universal, like music or writing, may be excluded or delayed in development. In a study of regularities, a perfect correlation would be surprising. We find forms of sculpture in all civilizations except the Islamic; writing in all except the Mexican and Peruvian; empires in all except the Mesopotamian, international systems in all except the Egyptian.

Without an awareness of recurrence, anomalies could not be perceived. But once they are seen, they raise questions that would otherwise have lain dormant. If Egyptian culture were the only one you knew, the idea of international relations within a civilization would never be considered. But when Egypt is viewed as one of ten cultures, we immediately ask why a system of city or nation states has failed to materialize. What was there in the culture patterns or external circumstances that caused this anomaly? Is there something else in the culture that performs the same functions? In Western civilization we are particularly attracted to events. We analyse and evaluate them. But we pay little attention to what did not occur. To waste time on what might have happened or what didn't happen is regarded as speculative, rather irresponsible, a needless and rather fanciful complication of the study of history. Before Spengler and Toynbee, the historian studied Europe as a system of sovereign states, the given condition of his inquiry. But it is perfectly respectable to ask why Europe is a system of states: is it a pattern like that of South-East Asia, or is it that the imperial phase has not yet been reached, as was the case in the Hellenistic period of Classical history or in India before the Mughal empire? It is only comparative study that uncovers anomalies, that calls our attention to what did not or has not happened.

Note

Industrial Recurrence

Recurrence at the civilizational level inevitably sounds mystical. But regularities within a civilization are taken for granted. The same patterns have repeated themselves over and over again in the industrial revolution, so that it is common for the élite of underdeveloped countries to speak as if they knew what would happen to their economy and their society, given the necessary capital and a certain level of integrity and competence in management.

5:   In Defense of Determinism

Comparative historians have been criticized frequently for their tendencies toward determinism: it implies omniscience about the future, it leads to rigid conceptions of time and space frequently expressed in absurd systems and charts, it frequently encourages attitudes of pessimism and hopelessness and it denies the individual the possibility of controlling his own destiny.

This concern about determinism and historical inevitability is possibly excessive.   It would be surprising, after all, if writers comparing conditions and forces were not inclined to emphasize developments beyond man's control.   But there is no denying that the existence of recurrent patterns implies the possibility of predicting the future.   As soon as you admit this, however, you are naturally expected to forecast the fate of your own civilization.   Spengler has done so.   He tells us that as he reads his data, we can look for its demise about 2200 A.D.   This gives his reputation a built-in three hundred year guarantee.   Sorokin knows not only what is going to happen but also how to help it along.   Toynbee has hesitated and hedged.   I can understand Toynbee's caution.   He doesn't want the result of all his learning and study to depend on his ability to predict the course of a single civilization.

Sometimes, to escape this dilemma, it is easier to deny all capacity for prediction.   Toynbee and Sorokin, between predictions, often do this.   But if you say you can't predict, you then have to explain what good comparative study is, what does it all come to?   This, by now, is a familiar question to any student of history.   It often happens, of course, that the most abstract studies prove to be the most pragmatic.   The student who concentrates on the comparative study of civilizations and their component patterns may contribute more to solving problems of foreign policy than a student who concentrates on the problems themselves.   He may.   It is not easy to guess about the practical results of generalized studies.   If you start guessing too early, you interfere with your own objectivity.

So the comparative study of civilizations may suggest a good deal about the future. But that is not its only justification.

A deterministic cast of thought, plus the fact that comparative historians have been dealing with the total study of history, have frequently led to the creation of rather rigid, dogmatic, all-embracing systems that seek to answer all questions for all time and to reduce history to a series of charts in which civilizations go through their paces with the predictability of well-trained circus animals. It would seem that systems which answer all questions as soon as they are raised might destroy the capacity of the historian to further develop his thinking. Take Spengler. He completed the *Decline* at the age of thirty-seven. In the nineteen years remaining to him he did little that mattered. If he had been more cautious, if he had suspended judgment, could he have not done more? It is hard to say. Those who do suspend judgment have a way of never coming to any conclusions at all. And meanwhile the systems provide a frame of reference, instead of closing off further investigation. It has been Spengler's very dogmatism that has been so stimulating, that has forced so many historians to rethink their positions.

Even more dogmatic are the charts that often accompany the systems of the comparative historians. But these charts must be accepted as models, and as such they must sacrifice accuracy for intelligibility; they must have an element of arbitrariness. It is no less reasonable to make a chart of a civilization cycle than it is to make a chart of a business cycle. And the comprative historian must chart the unknown, even though he is certain to err, just as the sixteenth-century cartographer was justified in making maps, even though they amuse us today.

Dogmatic systems and charts also serve to reduce the feeling of unreality that pervades the study of long-term recurrences. It is easy to believe in the recurrence of smaller events more closely interspersed, as in the recurrence of economic depressions. But recurrences of major patterns, not easily verifiable, and certainly not within the range of anyone's experience, tax credulity. Succinct charts serve to bring such long comparative sequences into the realm of intelligibility.

It is sometimes argued that the study of the decline and fall of civilizations reflects an unhealthy pessimism, a desire to surrender to the forces of history. Whether a writer's conclusions are "optimistic" or "pessimistic" is, of course, irrelevant. All you can ask is whether he has chosen his data judiciously and whether his conclusions logically derive from those data. Nor are the conclusions of comparative history entirely pessimistic. The concept of reconstitution has once and for all scrapped the picture of a civilization hurtling inevitably to its doom. Kroeber, in particular, has been assiduous in rooting out gloom-and-doom terminology. But for all this, there are strong strands of pessimism in the comparative studies of civilizations. In a nuclear world this pessimism seems to have considerable relevance. But a difficult situation can also be a challenging one. Men can and do rise to difficult situations. A knowledge of truth or a knowledge of the odds does not necessarily deter them. I should worry rather about the men who deny the dark side of life, the kings (or critics) who slay the bearers of evil tidings.

Conditions determine the kind of creative individual who can come to the fore. Kroeber in *Configurations of Culture Growth* seems to have proved conclusively that the realization of genius is not a matter of chance. Part of the greatness of a man lies in his ability to measure his circumstances, to make use of the political and economic institutions available to him. The study of history reveals the limitations of man, but it need not prevent him from acting. An understanding of historical patterns, far from discouraging man, may well encourage him to dare.

SOURCES

A. CULTURE CHANGE

Pitirim Sorokin, *Social and Cultural Dynamics,* abridged ed., Ch. 38, "Immanent Change"; Christopher Dawson, *Dynamics of World History,* pp. 3-11, "The Sources of Culture Change."

B. ORIGINS

Oswald Spengler, *The Decline of the West,* II: 33-38, the birth of culture; Arnold Toynbee, *A Study of History,* I: 271-299, "Challenge and Response"; A. L. Kroeber, *The Nature of Culture,* Ch. 1, "Explanations of Cause and Origin"; Dawson, *Religion and Culture,* Ch. III, "Relation Between Religion and Culture"; Rushton Coulborn, *Feudalism in History,* pp. 364-383, "Feudalism"; Coulborn, *The Origin of Civilized Societies,* Ch. 3, "The River Valleys"; Carroll Quigley, *The Evolution of Civilizations,* Ch. 3, "Groups, Societies, and Civilizations"; Karl Jaspers, *The Origin and Goal of History,* pp. 44-48, novel qualities of early civilizations.

C. CULMINATION

Spengler, *Decline,* I: 31-36, the problems of civilization; Toynbee, *Study,* IV: 1-5, "The Problem of Breakdown"; IV: 119-137, "The Failure of Self determination"; V: 1-15, "The Problem of Disintegration"; Sorokin, *Dynamics,* abridged ed., Ch. 39, "The Principle of Limit"; Kroeber, *Anthropology,* pp. 326-328, "Climaxes of Whole Culture Patterns"; *Configuration of Culture Growth,* pp. 763, 796-7, 813-825, culminations, reconstitution, cultural death; Quigley, *Evolution,* pp. 77-78, reform and circumvention; Flinders Petrie, *The Revolutions of Civilisation,* Ch. V, "Relations of Different Activities."

D. TOTAL CYCLES (Sections 2 and 3)

Spengler, *Decline*, II: Ch. IV, "The Soul of the City"; Sorokin, *Social Philosophies of an Age of Crisis*, pp. 239-241, "The Fallacy of One Life Cycle"; Sorokin, *Society, Culture and Personality*, Ch. 47, "The Life Span, Death and Resurrection of Cultural Systems"; Kroeber, *Configurations*, pp. 836-846, "Conclusions"; *An Anthropologist Looks at History*, Ch. 2, "Have Civilizations a Life History?"; Quigley, *Evolution*, Ch. 5, "Historical Change."

E. REGULARITIES

Spengler, *Decline*, charts between volumes, "Contemporary Spiritual, Cultural and Political Epics"; Toynbee, *Study*, IX: 338-348, "Are Laws Inexorable?"; VII: 327-331; VII: 569-576, charts on universal states and higher religions; *Study*, abridged ed., I: Table V following p. 566, total civilizations; Sorokin, *Dynamics*, abridged ed., Ch. 41, "The Reason for Super-Rhythms"; Kroeber, *Style and Civilizations*, pp. 149-160, "Conclusions"; Coulborn, *Feudalism in History*, pp. 383-395, uniformities; Morris E. Opler, "The Human Being in Culture Theory," *American Anthropologist* (June 1964, Part 1), 507-528; Julian Steward, *Theory of Culture Change*, pp. 87-92, the discovery of regularities through the use of the comparative method.

III

POLITICAL AND ECONOMIC PATTERNS

1: FEUDAL, STATE AND IMPERIAL PHASES

Thus far I have considered civilizations in terms of their general development. Now I would like to talk about the kinds of systems and patterns that make them up, and how their various phases of development relate to the whole. Obviously there are a tremendous number of intermingling patterns, and some kind of conceptual framework will be necessary in order to manage them. In this chapter, therefore, I shall concentrate on the political and economic aspects of civilizations that we stress in writing narrative history. In the next chapter I shall consider the ideas, the aesthetic reflections, the attitudes that give the civilization its meaning and color. Then we shall have the building materials for the construction of a model.

Civilizations seem to develop from a highly complex, personal, decentralized set of relationships that we in the West usually associate with feudalism. But feudal systems sooner or later tend to evolve into a simpler, more centralized and impersonal system we have come to call a state. If a number of states evolve in relation to one another, this might be called a state system. If one state gains hegemony over others, we say it has formed an empire. If the empire is central, but has relations with independent lesser states on its periphery, we might describe this system of relationships as an imperial system. Usually a feudal type of system appears in the formative stages of a civilization, or when it is recovering from a catastrophe. State systems usually occur next, but a civilization may oscillate between the state and imperial types of system several times, as has been the case in Chinese civilization.

In drawing a model, equal attention should be given to each of these phases, but we live in a state system that seems in many respects to be on the verge of transition, so it is not unnatural that we should be particularly interested in this phase. The comparative historians have been inspired to write because they believe the West is in this phase, and possibly this causes them to give disproportionate attention to it. This in turn may contribute to distortion in the model attempted here. The transitional phase tends to be drawn in excessive detail and the feudal and imperial systems seem to exist as prelude and epilogue to the state system as a whole. This is a distortion I can at this point recognise and modify but not eliminate. It may be that the twentieth century provides the historian with greater opportunities for detachment, but he still has to write from some standpoint. And it may be also that the state phase is really more interesting and important in many civilizations.

At some point most going civilizations have tended to articulate themselves, as Toynbee says, "into a system of mutually independent local states" (A Study of History, III: 301). It often seems that several such states arise from the same feudal system without reference to one another. Draco and Solon could concentrate on internal problems without worrying much about interference from Corinth or Spata, which had their own problems. The states of the Ch'un Ch'iu period in China long had only sporting relations with one another before their conflicts took a more serious turn. Obviously the same kinds of problem exist throughout large areas of the feudal system and the states represent attempts to solve these problems. Obviously the feudal system itself is in transition, and the political changes are going to be only one of many manifestations of this transition. The political system which is being broken up has been one of elaborate political relationships between lords and vassals. These relationships have been changing and unstable, they have often involved disruption and war to clarify power relationships, but if the system has survived at all, these unstable relationships must have provided enough protection to make the system coherent, and to enable it to function. The replacement of this system by another suggests that the feudal system has passed a culmination, that a reconstitution was necessary if ossification or disintegration were not to take place. The recurrent development of the state system in so many civilizations suggests that this is the most effective response to the existing challenge. Casting back a step further, it is apparent that the feudal system itself is the outcome of a still earlier challenge that arose either from the emergence of conditions that made primitive society impossible or from the disintegration of a previous civilization.

Once the states do come into existence out of the transforming feudal system, they begin to interact with one another. It is then possible to talk about international relations, although the powers may not be nations, but cities. At first their interaction may be peripheral and local, but as they develop, this interaction spreads until the states "coalesce into a single vortex drawing into itself the whole of the action in all quarters of the international arena" (Toynbee, *A Study of History*, IX: 261). In the process some burgeoning states may be eliminated by others, but ultimately a number of survivors reach an uneasy state of equilibrium. Each is sufficiently integrated and sufficiently powerful according to the techniques of the period to defend itself against any of the others, but none is powerful enough to subdue any of the others. (Normally defense has an advantage over offense in conflicts between states.) A balance of power has thus come into existence.

From time to time changes take place. New methods are developed whereby one state can increase its power in relation to others, or individual mischance leads one to become weaker. If one becomes more powerful, its neighbors are likely to seek one another's support in order to resist its power. The combining and shifting alliances tend to preserve the existence of any single state, and the managing of these alliances becomes the art of diplomacy. Since most of the relations between states will not be hostile, certain conventions will arise to expedite economic exchange and other relationships. An unwritten system of international law will develop. Certain actions between states will be recognised as supporting the system and others will be recognised as detrimental to it and therefore wrong. A system of international morality will develop. The longer the system is in existence, the more elaborate become its codes, and the more conscious men become of their existence.

This process represents a crystalization of the state system, a re-creation of the functions that served the feudal system, or in its prime, the feudal system was also characterized by codes of law and morality, methods of diplomacy and shifting systems of alliance. The thirteenth-century Western noble is implicitly lord or vassal to other lords, judge and protector to his peasants. The eighteenth-century king has fairly explicit rights and obligations to other kings and to his subjects. The Parthian noble and the Sassanian king after Shapur II are in similar crystalized positions. These are parallel political frameworks that support the same civilization in two different phases of development.

It may be that in a constellation of states one will arise that has sufficient power to challenge all the others. In this case the balance of power becomes a bi-polar alignment until either the threatening state has been reduced in power or it has conquered all the others. If the latter occurs, the balance of power comes to an end. So, of course, does the state system. The Assyrians and the Burmese were often challenging their respective systems, but never able to bring off a complete conquest. But every famous empire — the Maurya, the Inca, the Achemenian — came into existence because one group conquered all the others.

Mentuhotep began his reunification of Egypt from Thebes, far up the Nile. Shih Hwang-ti and Philip of Macedonia were considered semi-barbarians. It frequently seems to happen that the challenging state arises on the periphery of the system. This happens either because the central states limit one another too effectively while those in the peripheral regions are free to develop, or else because those in the center have passed the culmination of their development as states. It also happens frequently that more than one peripheral power develops in the same period. These may dominate the central states, but they cannot dominate one another. In that case a new and much larger state system succeeds the original. Thus the Greek city states served as a cockpit for the Hellenistic system and the Italian city states performed a similar function for modern Europe. The once peripheral European states seem themselves to have become politically inferior to still larger peripheral giants.

State systems reach culminations just as feudal systems do. Political and economic problems change, as do related ideas and attitudes. Ultimately a state system reaches the limits of its possibilities, and these limits can be sensed in the same way that art patterns can be sensed. The consciousness of these patterns, exhibited for instance in a concern for the preservation or recovery of bygone modes of law and diplomacy, is an indication that they are becoming strained. This concern is likely to be manifested in periods of war, revolution, challenged ideas and violent emotions. Even more than most periods of transition, it is likely to be a time of troubles. The absorption of a state system into a larger peripheral system or the conquest of all by one are two possible political resolutions of the conflict.

Federation, on the other hand, does not seem to work as a solution to the problems of a state system. Attempts to end conflicts within state systems have always proved less effective than imposed unity. Neither the eloquence of Demosthenes nor the threat of Macedonia could reduce the futility of various fourth century Greek leagues. Nor could Alexander I sensibly divide Europe with Napoleon on the raft at Tilsit. Even the five tiny Central American states couldn't work out a federation in the nineteenth century, and they were only repeating the story of the Mayapan League of the Middle American civilization. The balances and subtleties required apparently have been too delicate to manage in violent times.

If the state system is absorbed into a larger peripheral entity, what emerges may behave like a state system in a more crystalized phase. If one state conquers all the others, an empire will be created. The problems of empire are like those of a nation state developing out of a feudal system. Power must be consolidated, loyalty must be inculcated, insurrection must be subdued. How easily this is accomplished depends on the fortuitous skill of the government and on the vitality of the overturned state systems. If attitudes favoring the state system still exist, the empire may be short-lived, as in the case of Shih Hwang-ti's empire that was to last ten thousand ages, and the Asian empire of Alexander the Great. But often there has been a longing for unity, and the government finds general acquiescence if not strong support.

The empire, like the state, must be considered part of a system. Usually the system consists of one major political entity surrounded by many minor ones of varying levels of autonomy and culture. China usually had peaceful relations with one or more states in Korea and Manchuria, less peaceful relations with Tibet and the nomads of Central Asia, almost symbolic relations with the states of South-East Asia. Occasionally, as when the Delhi Sultanate had conquered northern India and Vijayanagar was unifying the south, two empires may be considered part of the same system. A group of states may acquire the characteristics of an empire, even though its political system contains a multiplicity of sovereign powers. Comparative historians tend to use variations of this explanation to account for the constant division of the Middle East. For although the political structure is extremely important, it is only one of many indicators of the existence of an imperial system.

An empire often succeeds in insuring a long period of political tranquility. It is managed by an efficient civil service that is likely to extend its control to provincial areas requiring it, or to allow a considerable measure of provincial government where inhabitants are willing and able to maintain it. Unfortunately even so stable and satisfactory-looking an institution as an empire begins to suffer erosion. The civil service begins to stifle its own effectiveness. The government is no longer able to cope with internal dissatisfactions or to protect its citizens from external attack. Once again a transitional phase takes place and if a reconstitution cannot be effected, either a rigid, totalitarian ossification must be maintained, or the government is replaced by private feudal systems until other civilizations, or even primitive cultures, overrun the shell that remains.

There is probably a tendency among those living in state systems for "realists" — those who give precedence to the "facts" of history — to believe that the balance of power, despite polarizations, is a basic political condition. The study of international relations may become important enough to distinguish from the study of politics or history. As the conflict between nations grows more intense, there may be a tendency among the "idealists" — those who believe that striving for "higher objectives" can overcome the facts of history — to believe that a completely new political order must come into existence, that the old balance of power must be obliterated once and for all, and that a new moral tone must come into existence in order to accommodate the changed society.

Likewise there is probably a tendency in imperial systems of long standing for the "realists" to believe that the world state, despite surface revolutions and disruptions, is a basic political condition. Instead of a study of international relations, there would be a study of world administration and law. As strains within the empire grow more intense, there may be a tendency among the "idealists" to believe that a time must come when the world order as it has been understood will come to an end, and that new and permanent values must be sought to replace those that are no longer tenable.

NOTES

a. Do Minor Powers "Stabilize" a State System?

Toynbee and Quincy Wright think that as a balance of power is achieved, more states can come into existence under the protection of this balance. The addition of these states, in turn, gives the balance greater stability and flexibility (Toynbee, *A Study of History*, IX: 236; Wright, *A Study of War*, II: 755-756). It seems to me, however, that there are usually only a few major states playing the power game and that the minor states serve the cause of "stability" only in that they can be used as gambits and trading materials. Moreover their presence can create the minor incidents out of which many unintended major conflicts can emerge.

b. Does Polarization Indicate Impending Unity?

Toynbee and Wright take the view that the demise of a state system is foreshadowed by repeated polarizations of power resulting eventually in the establishment of an empire (*A Study of History*, IX: 234-287; *A Study of War*, II: 760-766). This view is untenable. Polarizations are inherent in the balance of power at any stage of its existence; they are not confined to periods of disintegration. There are many examples: Egypt before the Old Kingdom, Athens and Sparta, the East Roman empire and the Sassanian empire, the Bahmini kingdom and Vijayanagar in Southern India, the Sung and Khitan empires in China.

c. Persistence of Political Forms

Toynbee observes in his *Reconsiderations* that "universal states are easily restored after short breakdowns and often restored, even by alien regimes, after long breakdowns" (see Coulborn, "Toynbee's Reconsiderations: A Commentary," *Journal of World History*, Vol. VIII: 26). I think that feudal and state systems also have a propensity toward reformation that is not easily suppressed. If a system has worked a long time, men will be reluctant to give it up. And when they do give it up, the subsequent hardships of life will glorify its memory and encourage them to support its restoration if the opportunity should arise.

2: A PRELIMINARY MODEL

The preceding section provides a basic political framework which can be related to other patterns of a civilization. But although I have tried to indicate periods in which a number of alternatives are possible, the overall impression of such a presentation is an inevitable progression from feudalism to empire. If I now repeat the process with war, government, economics and society, I shall only strengthen this deterministic impression. I should like to pause at this point, therefore, and construct a basic model with the material already presented, to indicate the wide realm of possibilities that exist for any developing civilization.

First of all, to recall Sorokin's terms, the development of all systems can be viewed as a fluctuation between crystalization and transition, between higher and lower periods of integration. As we saw periods of formation and periods of disintegration are both periods of transition, and both may be occurring at the same time. All periods of transition must lead either to a new crystalization or to a complete disintegration of the system. Each crystalization, because of the inherent process of change, must lead to another transition unless patterns become institutionalized and their forms ossify and become meaningless.

Suppose we represent these stages by the following letters:

C = Crystalization
T = Transitional stages (including formative)
D = Complete disintegration (the ashes, not the fire)
O = Ossification (freezing at a crystalized stage)

The following model represents all possibilities for a system:

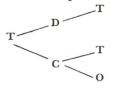

The T's must read as repeats. From each you go back to the beginning and start again. If I were to draw it all out it would extend infinitely off the page and look very like a diagrammatic representation of a complex molecule:

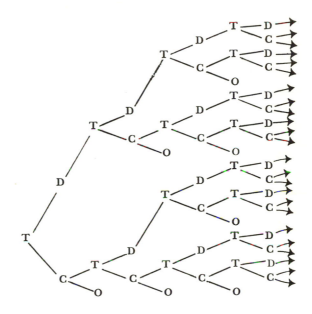

The D's pave the way for a new T, but it may not occur. The O's leave you stuck. They must become unstuck sometime, and probably proceed to D. But leaving them as dead ends illustrates them better.

Now let us apply this model of a system to the particular system we are calling a civilization. Let us substitute the symbols F, S and I for the feudal, state and imperial phases. And let P stand for primitive culture. Leaving out D's and O's for a moment, we get:

$$PC - PT - FC - FT - SC - ST - IC - IT$$

This is the set kind of primitive-to-empire evolution that we associate with Spengler, and it is the kind that tends to get underlined in these models. But it is not as simple as that. Apparent transitions may turn out to be premature, or a reconstitution may take place that permits a reversion. We must allow for that:

$$\begin{array}{ccccccc}
 & \text{PC}\cdot & & \text{FC}\cdot & & \text{SC}\cdot & & \text{IC} \\
 & \nearrow & & \nearrow & & \nearrow & & \nearrow \\
\text{PC} - \text{PT} & \text{FC} - \text{FT} & \text{SC} - \text{ST} & \text{IC} - \text{IT} & \text{FC}
\end{array}$$

Every transitional period can now lead to two alternatives, either an advance to the next succeeding stage or a reversion to the previous. But note that we are eliminating some possibilities A primitive society has never developed a state system without undergoing a feudal phase. And, if Coulborn is right, no civilized culture can return to a primitive stage. The loss of knowledge and history does not, or at any rate has not, extended that far. Any time a reversion occurs, as from FT to FC, the possibilities existing at the time of the previous condition are open again. It is rather like a pin-ball machine. The ball, when shot, has a universe of possibilities (the ball being the culture and the machine the universe), but as soon as it passes through the first slot on its downward curve, the possibilities are narrowed. Thus, having reached FC, it can no longer return to PC. But the machine also has rubber bumpers, so that the ball can reverse its course. Having reached slot SC, it can no longer return to PC, the initial ejecting slot, which has been closed off by a one-way valve.

We have still to add D's for total disintegration (back as far as the feudal level anyway) and O's for crystalized ossification:

$$\begin{array}{ccccccccc}
 & \text{PC} & & \text{FC} & & \text{SC} & & \text{IC} \\
 & \nearrow & & \nearrow & & \nearrow & & \nearrow \\
\text{PC} - \text{PT} & \text{FC} - \text{FT} & \text{SC} - \text{ST} & \text{IC} - \text{IT} & \text{FC} \\
 \searrow \text{O} & \searrow \text{D} \searrow \text{O} & \searrow \text{D} \searrow \text{O} & \searrow \text{D} \searrow \text{O} & \searrow \text{D} \\
 & \searrow \text{PC} & \searrow \text{FC} & \searrow \text{FC} & \searrow \text{FC}
\end{array}$$

After total disintegration it is probable that a reorganization will take place. If the disintegration takes place after a primitive transition, a primitive culture will emerge; if after any phase of a civilized transition, a civilized (feudal) culture will emerge.

This basic model of civilizations is subject to an infinite number of variations. It may look like this:

$$\text{PC} - \text{PT} - \text{FC} - \text{O}$$

which is what Toynbee would call an arrested civilization. Or it may look like this:

$$\text{FC — FT — SC — ST — SC — ST — IC — IT}\underset{\nearrow}{\overset{}{\diagup}}\text{FC} \quad \text{IC — IT}\underset{\searrow}{\overset{}{\diagup}}\overset{\text{IC}}{\underset{\text{FC}}{}}$$

which is the Russian Third Rome theory: from archaic Greece to the Greek city states to the Hellenistic period to the Roman Empire to Byzantium to the Russian Empire. Or it may look like this:

$$\text{PC — PT — FC — FT — IC — IT}\diagup\overset{\text{IC}}{\diagdown}\text{O}$$

which is a possible interpretation of Egyptian civilization, although it shows SC–ST skipped, which according to the model is not possible. I would guess that SC traces will be found if other than the political form is sought. Or it may look like this:

$$\text{IT — FC — FT — SC — ST}\diagup\text{SC — ST}$$

which approximates Western civilization (Quigley's view).

The model we consider in the remainder of this and the following two chapters tends to look like this:

$$\text{FC — FT — SC — ST — IC}$$

But the reader might try to keep the basic model in mind, even if the writer forgets it.

3: PATTERNS OF WAR

War appears to be a universal phenomenon. The forms of social structure that happen to exist only modify the form war will take. It may occur among a feudal nobility, among states, or between a civilization and barbarian cultures. It may be internal. But war in some form has been a normal phenomenon in all phases of a civilization (Richard Coudenhove-Kalergi, *From War to Peace,* pp. 24-25).

War is often a sign of vitality. Peoples who have the energy and the capability to wage war successfully often also have the energy and capability to accomplish much in other areas. Periods of great cultural achievement and chronic war are closely related in the histories of the Italian city states, Spain, England, the Netherlands and France. Men fight best, after all, if they consider there are values worth fighting for, and they seem to fight most violently if the cause is noble. Wars fought for the defense of a religion, or of a nation, tend to be more violent than those fought for partial political or economic advantages. Often it seems to take a war to raise men above the level of everyday petty strife, to see themselves as standing unselfishly for a greater unity.

But obviously war can also be a sign of disintegration. Accommodations which have been maintained between states in a crystalized system become less satisfactory and friction increases. The technology of a civilization, including its military apparatus, outgrows weakening political and social patterns and begins to have a destructive effect. The process of disintegration creates conflicts that lead to an increase in the violence and magnitude of war, and this increase in violence and magnitude accelerates the process of disintegration beyond any possibility of reconstitution (China after the collapse of the Han; India after the fall of the Gupta empire; Mexican civilization when the atrocities of the Aztecs were compounded by those of the Spaniards).

Periods of transition following the development of crystalized state systems may be the most violent of all, since states become most efficient vehicles for warfare. These periods, which Toynbee calls "times of troubles," have been identified by several comparative historians. They are characterized not only by violent encounters between states, but by appropriate related ideas and attitudes. Times of troubles have often been resolved by the establishment of an empire that brings the state system to an end, e.g. the Roman, Han or Achemenian empires. Often, but perhaps not always. It may be that a time of troubles is a particularly adaptable period, and when disintegration has gone far enough, a great man or a group of able men might shape it in several ways. The creation of an empire might be the most tempting solution to the problems that brought on the crisis, but alternative solutions, perhaps more subtle and difficult to achieve, might also be found, like the Western exploration and colonization following the Renaissance (and resulting ultimately in a different kind of empire), or the apparent Islamic adjustment to a pattern of continuous political fragmentation.

The presence of war, then, tells us little about the phase of a civilization. But the extent and duration of war in relation to the size of a civilization and the response of the civilization to the war tell us a great deal. Is the war incidental or consuming? Do men rebuild or do they restore? Is the civilization stimulated or is it devastated? These are the indicators by which the historian gauges the civilization's inner condition.

NOTE

The Destructive Function of War

War may perform those destructive functions that are essential in any period of transition, it may indeed clear the way for reconstitution. It may be, therefore, that an attempt to eliminate war in all forms forever would be misguided, or would lead to a delayed and much more severe and damaging conflict; it may be that men living in civilizations undergoing transformations would have more success if they tried to control war without eliminating it, if they permitted it to perform necessary destructive functions without allowing it to destroy the civilization itself.

In studying government, the first thing political scientists want to know is who holds the power: how is it divided between the leader and other members or permanent institutions of the government, between the government and the governed, between the center and the provinces?

In transitional times, the tendency is for power to gravitate to the center and away from the provinces, to the government and away from the governed, to a strong leader and away from other members or institutions. So Haremhab, by great exertion, reconstituted the Egyptian New Kingdom after it had been sorely tested by the reforms of Akhnaton; so Chao Kwang-yin had greatness thrust upon him by men who felt that only he could end the turmoil of the Five Dynasties period of Chinese history.

Crystalization, on the other hand, tends to bring about a wider distribution of power. The leader must consult others or reckon with permanent institutions and vested interests. The regions are allowed, sometimes encouraged, to handle their own affairs. Thus able consolidators like Amenhotep I of the Egyptian Middle Kingdom or Liu Pang of the early Han Dynasty, entering stable periods, were able to allow considerable autonomy to regional authorities.

The individual has his best chance for shaping a government to fit his own conceptions in periods when general cultural change has left the existing government an institutional anachronism. In such a period a determined man with a loyal personal following, a Caesar, may seize control of a state and use it for his own purposes. He maintains control not because he performs great deeds, but because he restores a sense of order. He performs a political reunification that corresponds to a desire for unity in other areas. He succeeds not because he is daring but because he is safe. He circumvents the old institutions and begins, regardless of his intent, to construct new ones that will be appropriate for a new civilization.

Spengler coined the term Caesarism to refer to the man who appears when the state system seems to be in transition. But early kings also performed the same unifying functions when the feudal system was in a corresponding phase. Ivan III and Ferdinand of Aragon devoted themselves to creating a personal following to be used against the established aristocracy. Henry VII and Louis XI performed similar functions for England and France. They were all feudal Caesars, succeeding because they were safe rather than daring, because they provided solutions that existing institutions no longer were capable of providing.

But try though he may, the great man cannot pass his decisive power to his successors. He creates institutions of his own — an administrative system, a system of laws, a financial system — which develop and relate to one another and to the culture for which they exist. Succeeding monarchs or emperors then find that they can achieve their ends only by using these institutions, not by circumventing them. Men can still become "great," but only in the way they use and represent the institutions, not by making new ones. Louis XIV or Hadrian play different roles from Napoleon or Alexander.

Despotic governments have been more frequent and more durable than representative governments. The lords of feudal systems are despots within their own domains. When feudal systems break up, one aristocrat subdues others and becomes a monarch. Those states in which the aristocracy retains power, like Poland, are likely to be overcome by their unified neighbors. And in later, more stable periods, if the positions of the monarchs have been undermined, they are likely to be replaced by tyrants whenever recurrent crises create a desire for a central authority that is capable of providing protection. Empires, of course, are usually founded and controlled by emperors.

It may be that freedom is a luxury that is less important and more abstract than other needs. It requires a population that is not only reasonably secure, but economically at least comfortable. It requires also a certain level of education. The concept of freedom is easily replaced by the concept of equality, because equality is more easily apprehended — it is easier to determine how well off you are in relation to your neighbors than whether your opinions are adequately represented in a distant government.

Moreover those who favor division and balance of governmental power have a more difficult task than those who prefer consolidation and simplification. The preservation of a representative government requires constant tinkering, the establishment of a despotism only one dramatic move. The maintenance of representative government requires a continuous adjustment of the instruments of government to constantly changing conditions. The establishment of a despotism requires only the destruction or circumvention of the troublesome instruments of government.

On the other hand, the concept of equality naturally encourages broadening the base of education, giving an equal opportunity to all citizens, and yet if this creates a literate but not particularly perceptive majority, it can be used by judicious employment of propaganda and press to create a strong basis of support for a totalitarian government. Thus education, a precondition for a stable republic, can also serve the cause of despotism. And the cause of equality can be served as well by a despotic government as by a republican government. Man can have equal rights, whether or not these include the right to vote. And both republican and despotic governments can be defenders of these rights, can serve to prevent men from usurping them from one another (Spengler, *Decline of the West*, II: 455-65; Toynbee, *A Study of History*, IV: 192-198; Sorokin, *Dynamics*, abridged ed., pp. 506-510; Albert Schweitzer, *The Decay and the Restoration of Civilizations*, pp. 15-21; Lewis Mumford, *The Transformations of Man*, p. 103).

Representative government, however, has been an anomaly in comparative history. It has occurred only in Classical and Western civilization, and then only during the state system phase. This raises the alternative possibility that its appearance as the dominant form in Western civilization (even in states in which the electorate actually has little power) heralds a new epoch in civilized history. This is a question that must be deferred until the elements of the civilization model have been presented and related.

NOTES

a. The Tendency Toward All or Nothing

There is a tendency in government toward totalitarianism or anarchy. The same holds true of rulers. Strong men become stronger and more intrusive until they stifle their own reigns (Louis XIV, Frederick the Great, Aurangzeb); weak men or a series of ineffective men leave problems unsolved until someone or something must take them in hand (Louis XV, the Russian Time of Troubles, the Ashikaga Shogunate). It seems most difficult for a man or a government to take a firm hold in order to allow internal freedom for development. Few have been able to achieve that kind of balance.

b. Can Governments be Reformed?

Comparative historians tend to argue that the problems of a civilization in transition cannot be met by governmental reform, since the problems lie not in government but in the culture itself. (Carroll Quigley, *The Evolution of Civilizations*, pp. 49, 59-60, 83-84, 239; cf. Sorokin, who thinks the more men tamper with institutions, the worse are the results they get: *Society, Culture and Personality*, p. 619.) But whether governmental reform is successful or not probably depends on whether it is relevant to the changes that are taking place in the culture. Reforms designed to create ideal, utopian governments probably will not be successful, but those that take into consideration changes in economic development, class structure and prevailing attitudes may very well effect a successful reconstitution. Governments, like other systems, can remain effective and relevant through internal adjustment or reform. The government of Great Britain transformed itself remarkably from the seventeenth through the nineteenth century; so did that of Rome as power passed from legislature to monarch; the government of the T'ang empire after An Lu-shan's rebellion was most completely restructured and redirected.

c. The Connotations of Bureaucracy

The term "bureaucracy" has acquired the connotation of a complex government that is losing its relevance, that exists more for its own sake, than for any purpose of operation. Before it reaches this decadent stage, or after it has been reformed, the same institution will be described as a civil service or a professional administration.

d. The Stability of Oligarchies

I have eliminated the term oligarchy from this section on the hunch that it may describe two kinds of administration. It may describe a group of "equal" leaders cooperating uneasily after a radical change in government, such as the Roman Triumvirate that followed Julius Caesar, or the French Directorate, or the interim Soviet governments that have followed the death or disgrace of a dictator. This kind of oligarchy is inherently unstable since it implies by its existence an uncertainty about the distribution of power. The other kind of oligarchy is the urban equivalent of the aristocracy. It develops with a leader and supports him, and if the ruling class is solidly entrenched it will last a long time. The urban rulers of Venice or the Netherlands would serve as examples. We might say that an oligarchy is inherently unstable if its power is purely political, but probably stable if it has an economic and social basis.

5: ECONOMIC PATTERNS

Economic patterns generally involve a breaking down of traditional land relationships in favor of an urban-centered economy, the development of specialization and interdependence, and an increase in wealth and standard of living. When a civilization becomes highly interdependent, it can also become highly vulnerable, and changes of economic fortune can come about suddenly. These economic crises can contribute, like militarism, to the disintegration of a civilization, but they cannot be said to bring it about.

When the agrarian patterns of a culture begin to break down, the culture loses something it never recovers. We all recognise this. We all find solace in vacationing on a farm or living in the country, in visiting our childhood homes and our families particularly during religious festivals like Christmas. Many of the ills of urban civilization can be traced to the lost solidarity of the agrarian period. But this solidarity involved what to an urbanite seems to be a harsh, onerous, tedious, narrow existence. It can be maintained only at the cost of early ossification.

The process of urbanization is difficult to describe without including the psychic factors that have been reserved for the next chapter. It involves not only a physical movement of people from the country to the city, but also a movement of ideas and ways of looking at things from the city to the country. As this economic orbit develops, villages that served as centers of economic trade and service are themselves served by country towns. Ultimately these towns in turn come into the sphere of influence of the more remote, exotic and attractive city. Some cities become great centers for nations as a whole, and the heartbeat of the nation seems to be embodied in that city. Eventually the process goes even further than that. The great cities become more alike, they outgrow the state they serve, the people who frequent them are at home in any of them but, as Spengler observed, alien even to the provinces of their native countries.

And ultimately, if the process is not checked, the cities seem to suck the country dry, to impose urban standards and forms on the country, and to leave the country towns and even the regional cities without any meaningful relation to their own environs.

The process of urbanization presumes a series of interrelated developments in agriculture, industry and commerce. There must be a partial transition from subsistence to cash crop farming or there could be no towns. If there is trade in the country, as Quigley points out, it is likely to take place between relatively distant regions, since those nearby would tend to produce similar crops. If there is industry, it is likely to consist of village crafts, mostly to serve the region, but possibly in exchange for desired luxuries from distant places. If the process of urbanization is to go very far, methods of farming must improve so that more people can be supported on the labor of one farm, or else a reduced agricultural supply must be made up by foreign trade: grain and other foodstuffs might be imported in exchange for special farm goods, craft products, or a combination of both, such as Athenian olive oil shipped to Egypt or Carthage in beautifully sculptured and painted vases. If the process goes far enough, there will be a demand for inventions to reduce the number of persons needed for farm labor, along with a migration of farmers to the city or to distant colonies, if these have been established to encourage trade. Inventions will also be applied to the improvement of industry, and part of the profits from enterprises will be retained for further expansion. Methods of production will become more elaborate, specialized, indirect. Some governments and some individuals will accumulate a great deal of wealth.

The processes described here will be accompanied by a change in the class structure of the civilization. Townsmen and merchants will become more important as the nobility and clergy decline. As peasants become displaced, they will wander to the towns where they will either become workers or rise to the middle class. Political advantages will lag behind economic status, and if sufficient concessions are not made by the nobility, the middle class, perhaps supported by the peasants and working class, will force its way into power, perhaps unseating the monarchy itself in the process.

As the process of urbanization continues, the nobility and clergy disappears, its surviving members becoming members of the middle class. The peasantry too, after supporting the middle class, is likely to be replaced by the proletariat — workers whose employment happens to be in factories instead of in fields. Neither the peasantry nor the proletariat ever becomes the governing class.

Though economic development may continue well into a period of disintegration, many factors are likely to bring it to an end. Of these the most important seem to be war, centralized political power, change in the nature of demand, agricultural exhaustion, the business cycle and the waning of materialism.

War seems to stimulate economic development for a considerable period since it encourages development of capital — accumulating industries, increases demand by the process of destruction and encourages improvements in technology. But the latter include improvements in weaponry until the amount of destruction taking place undermines the sources of production and destroys the desire to invest further capital. The more elaborate the civilization, the more difficult it is to destroy it, but also the greater is its capacity for destruction.

Though the central development of political power can serve to encourage production, it often winds up hampering private investment and destroying initiative. As government tends toward bureaucracy it is liable to intervene more and more, with a consequent loss of understanding of local problems and with an increasingly overintegrated and therefore fragile system. Every time production fails in one area, many others are affected, and a chain reaction is under way.

But even if capable leaders recognised the dangers of centralization, even if they managed to encourage individual initiative while maintaining high levels of employment and production, and even if leadership of this capability were to be maintained for centuries, problems would arise concerning the nature of demand. For once basic demands are met, civilizations have tended to seek luxuries, products not essential to the basic culture pattern, and products that do not in themselves favor further production. The acquisition of wealth, of course, makes a civilization a more desirable target for external attack and the softening effects of luxury make the citizens less capable of defending themselves.

As the movement to cities continues, and population increases, farms are cultivated more intensively to meet the increased demand. This sometimes leads to overcultivation of farmland, especially where one cash crop is produced. Civilizations may also tend to over-exploit other resources, so that men have to forage even further for wood or gold or coal to maintain the standards they have set for themselves. Thus far no civilization has perished because of over-exploitation of resources, though it has been a major factor in the decline of nations.

As patterns of specialization and trade develop, the civilization becomes more susceptible to internal breakdown. Industry becomes particularly susceptible to changes in demand, and any slackening can create an increased cutback in markets for basic industries — those that produce the materials that are to be used for further production — as intermediate sellers use up their inventories. This slackening can produce unemployment which in turn can lead to a further fall in demand as well as increased internal violence. Problems of this kind appear to have affected Italy as early as the second century A.D. and Constantinople after the loss of Asia Minor to the Seljuks in the eleventh century. The phenomenon of the business cycle is probably not restricted to Western civilization.

Finally economic decline may come about from a general change in attitude. Materialism runs its course until demands become insatiable and there is no possibility of satisfying them. Then an undercurrent of anti-materialism arises, and the best minds begin to question the importance of economic well-being. When even the establishment becomes involved with religious and philosophical speculation, as happened in the case of such famous monarchs as Akhnaton, Asoka and Constantine, investors and producers are likely to be discouraged. The precipitous decline that followed such monarchs as these may indicate a widespread indifference to material problems.

These economic declines are arrested either by the creation of a new political framework that opens up new market possibilities, or by a return to feudal-manorial patterns that abandon specialization, exchange and high living standards.

The relation between political and economic patterns should by now be fairly evident. But these physical patterns could not be discussed without recourse to words like "materialism" and "nationalism" that describe a collective frame of mind that cannot be subjected to statistical analysis. Before attempting the construction of a model, it is necessary to orient these psychic patterns.

Notes

a. Economics as a Phase Indicator

Comparative historians differ widely on the place of economics in the rise and fall of civilizations. Quigley and Shepard Clough concur with Marx in giving modes of production and distribution the determining function in development. Toynbee and others find economic growth still occurring while a civilization is in decline. Toynbee believes economics is an undependable indicator, since production is going on all the time in any culture. (Clough, *The Rise and Fall of Civilizations*, Chapter I; Quigley, *The Evolution of Civilizations*, Chapter 5; cf. Toynbee, *Study*, IX: 245; Sorokin, *Social and Cultural Dynamics*, abridged ed., p. 531; Dawson, *Enquiries into Religion and Culture*, p. 282; Spengler, *The Decline of the West*, II: 345, 401-402, 431-432).

b. Centralizing Forces in Mature Civilizations

The centralizing forces seem to be very strong in the latter phases of civilizations. If governments will not or cannot assume the centralizing functions, economic agencies will. Neither the local political leader nor the small businessman or farmer seems able or willing to stand against these forces. In the end what local vitality remains is directed toward the encouragement of intervention by big business or big government. The ablest men find their opportunities in the bigger operations and only the less able, those who for lack of ability or opportunity could not make the grade, stay at home.

Sources

A. Political Phases

Oswald Spengler, *The Decline of the West,* Table III, bound between the two volumes; "Contemporary Political Epochs", II: Ch. XI, "State and History"; Arnold Toynbee, *A Study of History,* IX: 234-87, "Struggles for Existence Between Parochial States"; III: 209-306, "Machiavelli" (the section indicated is not about Machiavelli but about his times, and the theory of peripheral domination is here adumbrated) ; Kenneth Thompson, *World Politics,* VIII: 374-392, "Mr. Toynbee and World Politics"; Quincy Wright, *A Study of War,* II: Ch. XX, "The Balance of Power"; Jacob Burckhardt, *Force and Freedom,* Ch. IV, "The Crises of History"; Rushton Coulborn, *Feudalism in History,* Part Three, "A Comparative Study of Feudalism"; Carroll Quigley, *The Evolution of Civilizations,* Ch. 5. "Historical Change in Civilizations."

B. Patterns of War

Spengler, *Decline,* II: IX, "State and History"; Toynbee, *Study,* IV: 465-505, "Suicidalness of Militarism"; VII: 318-344, "Standing Armies"; IX: 473-561, "Technology, War and Government" (in the West) ; Pitirim Sorokin, *Social and Cultural Dynamics,* abridged ed., Part VI, "Fluctuation of War"; Wright, *Study of War,* I: IX, "Fluctuations in Intensity of War"; Kroeber, *Configurations,* pp. 670-1, 705-6, 715, correlations between war and cultural development.

C. Patterns of Government

Spengler, *Decline,* II: Ch. XII, "Philosophy of Politics"; Toynbee, *Study,* V: 35-58, "Dominant Minorities"; VII: 1-47, "Universal States as Ends"; VII: 80-239, "Imperial Installations";

Sorokin, *Dynamics,* Ch. 28, "Fluctuation of Government";
Wright, *Study of War,* II: XXII, "Conditions of Government
and War."

D. PATTERNS OF ECONOMICS

Spengler, *Decline* II: XIII and XIV, "The Form World of
Economic Life," X: "The Problem of Estates"; Toynbee, *Study,*
V: 58-194, "Internal Proletariat"; IX: 223-234, "Laws of Nature
in Economic Affairs"; Sorokin, *Dynamics,* Ch. 31, "Fluctuation
of Economic Conditions"; Shepard Clough, *Rise and Fall of
Civilizations,* pp. 1-19, the relation of economic and cultural
development; Coulborn, *Feudalism in History,* pp. 288-324,
"The End of Feudalism"; Quigley, *Evolution* Ch. V, "Historical
Change in Civilizations."

IV

INTELLECTUAL AND
EMOTIONAL PATTERNS

1: ATTITUDES TOWARD THE WORLD

People undergo collective emotional changes that correspond to the physical changes that take place within their culture. While individuals may feel favorably or unfavorably disposed toward aspects of their culture on any given day, an overall consistency in collective attitudes can be discerned in cultures as a whole. These attitudes do not lend themselves to measurement. We can only say that if certain sets of attitudes exist, certain physical consequences can be expected.

Thus we may expect that worldliness would increase with the process of secularization. Secularization, after all, is a transfer of primary concern from the spiritual to the material, from God to man. We may expect spiritual concerns to be higher in a feudal period and to decrease as secularization takes place. Whenever material solutions fail to work, however, we may expect a return to spiritual solutions. We might look for contrary reactions in periods of transition to whatever failed in a crystalized, integrated period. Therefore if spirituality leads to a failure to solve material problems of the feudal period, we might look for an increase in materialism in the transition to a state system. Material concerns, however, cannot all be satisfied in any culture, especially since the partial satisfaction of physical wants tends to create further physical appetites. These can be satiated in two ways: individuals can either devote an increasing amount of their time to satisfying their personal needs, thereby reducing the amount of time they devote to, say, community activities; or abandon as hopeless the attempt to satisfy their increasing material needs and concentrate primarily on spiritual development. Thus a man, frustrated by the failures and difficulties of political life, might quit office, and spend more time either promoting investments and improving his golf game, or studying philosophy and performing community services. Ultimately, of course, if too high a percentage of men become preoccupied with material consumption, and not enough are engaged in government and the hard work of economic production, the material needs of the individual will not be satisfied anyway. Or even if they are satisfied, he may find his life hollow, empty, lacking "spiritual" qualities. In that event he may go to a psychiatrist and attempt to understand his own way of looking at things, he may decide that "money isn't everything" and pursue ideas instead, he may become more devoutly religious. A widespread loss of faith or interest in an economic system may render a civilization economically inoperative. In that case, if it is not overcome by external powers, the system may break down, and men will have to live as best they can with what food they can procure or grow. If they try to procure it by buying or stealing, they will ultimately create a tremendous inflation and perish. If they try to grow their own, they will accept a great reduction in living standard and return to a feudal system. If the reaction against material failures leads to a reconstitution of the political system, a new period of material success may ensue and spirituality can then be expected to decline. The majority of people in any culture can be expected to accept physical comfort and still more physical comfort as an adequate end.

If this hypothesis is valid, we might expect a feudal period to be one of spiritual concern, the transition from feudalism to be one of increasing materialism, the integrated state system to be predominantly materialistic, the transition from the state system to be extremely materialistic but with an increasingly vehement minority rejection of materialism. If an imperial system is established, we might expect a return to moderate materialism. If the imperial system is challenged, we may again expect a recurrence of extreme materialism and increasing spirituality. If the state or imperial system remains in transition over a long period, spirituality will increase and materialism decline to minimum necessity. Under such circumstances a feudal system is likely to emerge. This was the case in Europe for a millennium after the fourth century A.D., and in India for a similar period, beginning with the spread of Hinduism during the fourth and fifth centuries, while the Gupta empire was still dominant.

Materialism is not synonymous with material welfare. It includes a whole complex of philosophies and ideas that have to do with the world as it is, the lessons of history, the empirical approach. Realism and rationalism, utopianism and pragmatism are all materialistically-oriented approaches. Empiricism obviously has to do with testing ideas in the real world: what works is valid. Realism and rationalism appear to be opposites, since the political realist tries to see the world as it is while the political rationalist tries to see it as it could be. But both are materialistic in that they concentrate on what man does (or could do) with his own powers. Utopianism — really systematized rationalism, however grandly conceived — seeks a materialistic heaven. Pragmatism can serve the cause of materialism in both integrated and transitional periods. In an integrated, materialistic period it has to do with preserving or developing things as they are. In a disintegrating, materialistic period it is concerned with getting along in spite of conditions.

Even when materialism as such is challenged, this does not necessarily mean the beginning of a trend toward spirituality. In the nineteenth century the fruits of materialism were taken for granted. In the twentieth century, materialism is being challenged. Joseph Schumpeter, for one, takes a serious view of this challenge since it was materialism that made the industrial revolution possible. But if the organization man prefers comfort to accumulation, if the successors of Freud and Marx succeed in knocking the props out from under rationalism, and if nuclear war is capable of destroying the material structure, doesn't this indicate the onset of a spiritual revival? Possibly, but probably not. What is happening, rather, is an increasing consciousness of the concept of materialism. The quaint idea that money isn't everything is rather overwhelmed by sophisticated measurements of gross national products and development of the underdeveloped. The Freudian approach can be seen as the ultimate in rationalism: the rational consideration of the irrational. We shall see in discussing attitudes toward the state and toward form that a movement from the unconscious to the conscious is recurrent in the development of attitudes.

The more extreme materialism of transitional periods is likely to be accompanied by "spiritual" responses that turn away from materialism. One aspect of this spiritual response involves a reaction against excessive fragmentation brought about by rational, empirical analysis. This response seeks instead to find internal unity and higher meaning in what appears to be fragmentary and diversified. The writings of Western comparative historians themselves would seem to illustrate this pattern. A more extreme aspect of the spiritual response is to look for higher meaning not within the material world, but outside it.

The spiritual response is also brought about by a feeling that standards of morality have been abandoned. If people are concerned only about their own welfare, they do not care about others except in so far as it is pragmatic to be concerned. And if they are urbane, impersonal and rational, they are likely to repress their emotional development. The rational world is likely to be impersonal and unfeeling. The individual in it may feel lost, desperate, lacking in any justification for existence beyond his own well-being. Hence there is a strong need for synthesis, for making sense out of the diverse, for finding meaning in the whole.

No culture is going to be devoid both of material and spiritual concerns, and of individuals that seem to be primarily concerned with one or the other. The appearance of single signs is therefore not likely to be significant. Nor is the process from material to spiritual irreversible. The very breakdown of material patterns encouraged by the spiritual response may bring about a refocusing on the material world, a rebuilding of patterns in a different way, and perhaps a reconstitution of the culture. If that occurs, the spiritual patterns may serve to knit the culture, performing the function of religion in the phase of origin. The resemblances between periods of origin and periods of revival, observed by Coulborn, are relevant here.

The depth and extent of a spiritual response will also depend on basic culture patterns. Some cultures, like the Greek, are more worldly than others. The spiritual response will be of only marginal importance in some cultures, but crucial in others.

NOTES

a. Polar Meanings for "Realism"

It is a commentary on the times that the term "realism" as we use it today refers to the deriving of concepts from empirical observations of the behavior and interaction of things. Originally realism referred to the belief that ideas were "real" and things only reflections of ideas. The man who believed that things were real and ideas only names was called a nominalist. But we live in a nominalistic age.

b. The Bowler Continuum Applied to Attitudes

The Bowler Continuum, employed earlier to describe fluctuations of form, can also be used to describe fluctuations in attitudes. Thus Sam Jones, sitting in church, may concentrate alternately on the sublime love of God and the temporal beauty of Susie Smith, sitting in a summer frock, two rows down and to the left. His attitudes during the sermon might be transcribed like this:

TOTAL MATERIAL CONCERN

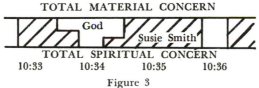

TOTAL SPIRITUAL CONCERN

10:33   10:34   10:35   10:36

Figure 3

But if the concerns of Sam Jones, and all others who have lived in his culture over a period of several centuries, could be collectively placed on such a continuum, we should possibly get something like this:

TOTAL MATERIAL CONCERN

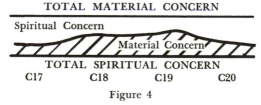

TOTAL SPIRITUAL CONCERN

C17   C18   C19   C20

Figure 4

We should then say that the nineteenth century was more materialistic than the seventeenth. We might simplify by saying that the nineteenth century represented a materialistic age, the seventeenth century did not.

I have noticed subsequently that this application of the Bowler Continuum to materialism and spirituality closely resembles Sorokin's chart of material and ideal fluctuations throughout the past two and a half millenniums (*Social and Cultural Dynamics*, abridged edition, p. 289). Sorokin's attempted measurement of these fluctuations shows a lower percentage of materialism than my smooth-curved guess. Perhaps this indicates how difficult it is for an inhabitant of a predominantly material culture to guess what a spiritual culture might have been like.

2: ATTITUDES TOWARD SOCIETY

We would expect that each phase of a civilization would be associated with prevalent attitudes toward the situation that exists. In crystalized phases we would expect loyalty to the manor, the state or empire. In transitional phases we would expect alienation from the society that exists and a search for something else.

The term nationalism describes an attitude related to the nation state. Since it arises from a general consciousness of achievement, since it is one of many manifestations of cultural relationship, its appearance would seem to indicate developing integration. In this situation it is inwardly and unconsciously developed as a logical prevailing attitude for a state system. The nationalism of sixteenth century England or of the seventeenth century Netherlands would be examples of nationalism of this kind.

If, on the other hand, nationalism is a political attitude formed by an intelligentsia and transmitted to other members of a culture, it is probably an indication of disintegration. The original nationalism has lost its function — its "charm," Toynbee would say. It is replaced by a kind of artificial social hormone, consciously developed and imitated by marginal areas of the civilization that have not been closely integrated in the earlier phase. The nationalism of nineteenth-century Europe or twentieth-century Africa would be examples of this kind.

In order to distinguish the two types, I am going to call the first developmental nationalism, the second derivative nationalism.

In a feudal society we do not think very much about loyalty to the feudal unit. These loyalties are based on practical considerations and the amount of force at the disposal of various feudal lords. Loyalties are much more strongly centered on the land that provides or denies subsistence, the family that controls the land, and through these the all-pervading religion of the times. The land and family are concrete and immediate. The deeper feelings of religion are expressed and understood through symbols.

Nationalism can emerge only when the religious impulse has weakened. It is a logical product of secularization. We first find loyalty extending beyond the family in the city state. In fact loyalty to the city perhaps exceeds all other secular loyalties because the city doesn't need symbols, it is a symbol. It is surrounded by walls. Leaders within these walls are acquainted with a large percentage of their followers. But for the loyalty really to take hold, for the fullest development of a collective identity, there need to be other cities. The Florentine and the Venetian are each sharply characterized for us partly through what they were to each other.

At the state level nationalism requires more. There are no walls, there is no possibility of seeing the state. There is no possibility of leaders knowing more than a small percentage of the state's citizens. So the first requirement for nationalism is the development of the concept of the nation. This takes a considerable period of time, it requires the breaking down of rival sources of loyalty such as a deity or a feudal lord. The religious symbols must be supplemented or replaced by symbols of the nation state like the crowned king and the national banner as well as history that gives a sense of tradition, justification, development, purpose. The development of nationalism, as in the case of the city state, is supported if other nations are developing in opposition. England needs France. Even China needs the non-Chinese barbarian. In both city state and nation there is an economic unity that helps strengthen the concept of nation. The correlation need not be exact, but it helps if the boundaries of a nation have economic justification. A common language, like a common economic system, also helps conduct the concept of a nation and define its boundaries. The Phoenicians shared language and economy, though their cities remained separate political entities. They even incurred considerable risk in refusing to join the Persian Emperor Cambyses in his campaign against distant Carthage, simply because their ancestors had founded the city several centuries earlier.

Derivative nationalism does not develop of itself, it is created. It is first apprehended among the intelligentsia, then among the better educated. With it comes artificially created history which is purposefully taught. Derivative nationalism seems to thrive on a degree of literacy not required by developmental nationalism. In Western civilization we know that the concept of nationalism was carried from the cities to the rural areas in central and eastern Europe only after the revolution of 1848. It penetrated deeper with the extension of education in the latter part of the nineteenth century and last of all a new intelligentsia was created in the marginal areas of the civilization, thus bringing about still another burst of derivative nationalism in the twentieth century. But similar artificial creations have been attempted before, as when Cyrus posed as the upholder of the Chaldean gods, or when the founder of the Gupta empire adopted the name Chandragupta because the founder of the earlier Mauryan empire bore that name. Both the Persian and the Indian leaders were creating artificial loyalties to a larger political entity.

Nationalism is a sturdy development, but it is liable to erosion by either victory or defeat, excessive familiarity or excessive remoteness, the destruction of internal pressures or the withdrawal of external pressures. The symbols and forms may live on long after the spirit has waned.

Nationalism declines because of the breakdown of the factors that made it possible. The secular loyalty is undermined. The history, under empirical study, is found to be mythology. The economic area, through peaceful contacts in the international system, has spread beyond the state. Languages become mixed and diluted as communications and transportation improve. A perception of common interest in the entire area leads to a growing tide of universalism — the perception of a brotherhood of man, a transference of loyalty to mankind. Common qualities among nations are emphasized, differences reconciled. Tolerance of alien viewpoints increases. Loyalty to the nation wanes. Lacking loyalty, governments must either increase compulsory measures or watch their defense capacity disintegrate. Often armies, strong in divisions and armaments, simply melt away when a conflict takes place. Improved transportation and the changing spirit lead to an increase of diplomatic interchange, particularly at higher levels. Economic treaties — reducing trade restrictions, tariffs and quotas — appear more frequently. Such were the characteristics of the Hellenistic states before unification, of China toward the end of the Six Dynasties period, possibly of Europe toward the end of the twentieth century.

Alliances and federations are often discussed and even tried, but when a strong power appears, or when one nation retains its old national loyalties a little longer because of its later cycle of development, world conquest takes place with relative ease. The Macedonians had little trouble with Greek alliances and federations, nor the Aztecs with the Mayapan. The Phoenicians survived the expansion of the Assyrian Empire by avoiding alliances opposing it. Loyalties are transferred from cities and nations to empires. The new loyalties are not so strong: the empire is more difficult to convey by symbols than was the nation and it lacks the stimulation of opposing nations. But an empire, if it cannot command love, at least may be admired, respected or tolerated as a necessary evil.

Neither peace nor the world state has anything like the rallying appeal of war and the nation. War involves action, its very appearance relieves tension. Consider the widespread popular enthusiasm for World War I in Europe after four decades of peace. And the nation has a tremendous advantage in having a concrete, representational opponent. All that a world state can stand against is the concept of war. After a period of uncreative peace, this becomes meaningless. Men become bored with peace, particularly if they have not experienced war.

Any major change requires apathy toward what exists. Change cannot take place if men are moved to rise up to defend the old order. It is when men prefer order, any order, that peace becomes possible. But still it has to be brought about by someone, and then it has to be administered. Federations require a balance, a careful and continuous working out of relationships, considerable patience and vitality. Empires require only general acquiescence. No wonder empires have succeeded and federations have generally failed.

The costs of peace have tended to be high. The price might be slavery, or at least the loss of most civil rights (and responsibilities). A government dedicated to order at any price may be expected to sacrifice the economic welfare of its subjects, since economic development implies a certain amount of political flexibility and upheaval. It may be expected to suppress any kind of aesthetic expression that could upset order, preferably all artistic expression since it is difficult to distinguish which may turn out to be dangerous. And though its subjects are protected against external war, they cannot be protected against arbitrary injustice and violence that may occur in the process of pursuing the central end of the society. So the peace bought at any price may not bring about a life particularly worth having. The value of life, both for the peasant and for much of the potentially creative elite, must have been greatly reduced in such tightly managed empires as the Maurya, the Ptolemaic, the Inca or Romanov Russia.

At no time in history has life been secure. It is not likely to be. The concentration on peace, like the concentration on materialism, represents an imbalance, a distortion of life. Any such imbalance is likely to mean that any achievement is reached only at great cost, a cost that from most other standpoints would seem to be unacceptable.

In a period of waning nationalism, government persists because of its utility rather than because of the loyalty it commands. The governed obey its laws because they want an orderly society, because they are accustomed to obeying and because they are not sufficiently distressed to seek an alternative. If the edicts of such a government are evaded, the evader may have no sense of sin. He may, for instance, feel pride in underpaying his taxes, he may tell his friends about it and receive praise for his cleverness. But he still wants the protection the government gives him and he does not contemplate getting along without it, as men do when they resort to feudalism in periods of declining empire.

A government in this position may maintain itself by force over an unwilling populace, or may try to bend the populace to its will by control of communications media. Such a government may have the tolerance of inhabitants who hope for nothing better from its overthrow. The perpetuation of such a government may lead to political apathy, a turning of interests away from society at all levels. Tendencies toward materialism and spiritualism will thereby be reinforced.

In the period in which loyalty to the government is waning, there is an increasing struggle on the part of the government to hold things together. As Toynbee puts it, a creative minority that led by "charm" is replaced by a dominant minority that controls by force. We can imagine these leaders frantically trying to bolster up the old order, bitter because people seem

to have lost their sense of responsibility, certain that they are
the last defenders of truth and righteousness. In the end they
are overturned not by the apathetic people but by the unscrup-
ulous Caesar who lacks any sense of service or righteousness, who
promises all things to all men, and who in fact turns the government into an instrument to support his personal ends.

Historians frequently associate adherence to ideologies with
violence in warfare. Thus the wars of religion and nationalism
are believed to have been more violent than the wars conducted
by barons or kings with mercenary soldiers for limited objectives. This assumption, I think, needs some modification. The
period of crystalized religion was the Middle Ages, the period
when wars were fought only when other business was not at
hand. The period of developmental nationalism was a period
of professional wars on land and commercial wars at sea. The
violent religious wars were fought during the Reformation,
when the old religious synthesis was breaking up. The violent
wars of nationalism date from the French Revolution, when the
challenge to the Western state system began. The Italian city
states, though given to viciousness and underhanded activity,
were notoriously tame when it came to warfare, as Machiavelli
lamented. In other civilizations, periods of decline and periods
of formation have been notoriously violent. Such was the period
of the Assyrian Wars, during the decline of Mesopotamia, or of
Far Eastern civilization from the time the T'ai-ping Rebellion.
So too was the period of anarchy in the third century A.D.,
preceding the formation of the Byzantine civilization, or the
period of nearly unrecorded conflict in India before the Mus-
lims began to restore order at the beginning of the second
millennium A.D. In other words, it is the challenge to and
widespread doubt about the prevailing ideology, that leads to
extreme violence. Widespread adherence to an ideology like
Christianity or nationalism leads to accommodation and peace.
This is true even in state systems because the idea that the state
is supreme implies the right of others to hold similar ideas about
their own states. The traitor is held in contempt even by those
to whom he gives information and help.

The relation between ideologies and cultural integration provides a clue to a problem arising from the concept of tolerance.
For if tolerance refers to the degree to which alien ideas are

permitted, we should expect intolerance in highly religious or nationalistic peoples, and growing tolerance in times of transition when religious or nationalistic ideologies are being challenged. Yet we have just pointed out that a state system can become integrated only when the idea becomes prevalent that other states within the system also have a right to exist. So it would appear that in this case a highly integrated period requires a high degree of tolerance.

The answer to this paradox would seem to be that just as there are two kinds of nationalism, there are also two kinds of tolerance. Or more accurately, the word "tolerance" is understood in two different ways. In an integrated system there must be accommodation. Differences are accepted, but they need not be understood. The fact that you belong to a different state does not threaten the existence of my state or my relation to it. The fact that you hold ideas that sound strange to me does not mean that I am going to try to argue you out of them or fight with you about them. I might shrug my shoulders and say everyone has a right to his own opinion. This is a closed-minded kind of tolerance. You live with alien ideas within your own culture because they don't threaten you, but you don't trouble yourself about trying to understand them. But if you find your own state or your own ideas being crowded by others, you will fight to defend your own.

The second kind of tolerance is an open-minded kind, occurring in periods of transition. It presupposes that there is no issue so certain or so important that a compromise cannot be effected. Anyone unwilling to compromise is considered stubborn, unreasonable, fanatic. This kind of tolerance places a premium on existence and no idea is worth its sacrifice. But many alien ideas are entertained. The tolerant person may be tolerant because he is uncertain of his own position, and hopes that something new will help him resolve the uncertainty. Once he finds something that does seem to help this resolution, he may abandon his tolerance and cling with unreasoning singleness of purpose to that idea. Thus the attempt of one generation to understand an intruding culture may become a fanatical nationalism in the next generation which is applying these ideas to its own problems.

One of the most baffling relationships is that between aesthetic development and attitudes toward a society. The interaction between developing nations often seems to produce accompanying aesthetic florescence. The great age of Spanish culture was also the age of Spanish power and expansion. Roughly. But on closer inspection the great period of expansion comes to an end in the latter half of the sixteenth century while the aesthetic period is just beginning. On the other hand the Elizabethan period and the development of Dutch painting do coincide closely with periods of conscious national pride and political greatness. One of the difficulties may be that it is not easy to establish the existence of political vitality. A great state may owe its existence to the lack of national will to resist while very small city states may be throbbing with national vitality. It may be that in the case of Spain the impulse that produced the great Spanish state also produced, with the ripening of time, the Spanish artists while the Dutch pattern, being smaller and simpler, ran closer together. It may be that the patterns of a civilization, and particularly the nature of the secularizing religion, affects the extent and kind of aesthetic vitality manifested in a period of developing nationalism.

NOTES

a. City States and Nation States

I have all through this section made little distinction between city states and nation states. Clearly city states are not nations, but they do have the same qualities as those found underlying nationalities: secular loyalty, hostility to other units in the system, common economic and language systems. If they are less strong on symbols and history, this may be because these are less needed for maintaining the state image. So even though they cannot be said to be subject to nationalism — indeed nationalism dealt the final blow to the Italian system — city states do behave like nation states, and both can be considered collectively as state systems.

b. How Universal Conscription Weakens the Nation

The extension of derivative nationalism and the increasing determination of a harassed dominant minority lead to the introduction of universal conscription. But universal conscription leads to the introduction into the ranks of men who particularly hate military life, including the intellectuals and writers who can express themselves on the subject (at least since the time of Napoleon in the West). So where the intelligentsia had once served to develop the national idea, at a later phase it serves to destroy it through anti-war stories and peace leagues. This contributes to a growing unwillingness to defend the colors and a contempt for patriotism.

c. The Spanish and Dutch Aesthetic Patterns

I wrote rather dogmatically about the coincidences of political power and aesthetic vitality. In the case of Spain, the political rise begins with the marriage of Ferdinand and Isabella in 1474 and the beginnings of decline are marked by the unsuccessful Dutch wars of the latter half of the sixteenth century, the defeat of the Armada in 1588 and the death of Philip II ten years later. But El Greco, the first and greatest of Spanish painters, is not active until the last quarter of the sixteenth century. Cervantes does not write Don Quixote until 1605. The flow of Spanish painting and literature continues until the death of Murillo and Calderon in the last quarter of the seventeenth century. The Spanish Golden Age, in other words, follows the defeat of the Armada.

The Dutch pattern is tighter. The revolt against Spain begins in 1566. Simultaneous, protracted wars against France and England in the latter half of the seventeenth century mark the beginnings of decline. From the eighteenth century on, the Netherlands are a third-rate power. Hals, the first great Dutch painter, is born in 1580. Hobbema, the last, dies in 1709. Rembrandt, the greatest, flourishes in the middle of the seventeenth century.

3: ATTITUDES TOWARD MAN

Men have always lived in groups. Man is a herd animal, like the deer, not a solitary like the fox. But whereas most animals have only seasonal disorientations, like the rutting season, man has cultural disorientations as well. We should expect, from what has already been said, that in periods of integration men would succeed in getting along with one another pretty well. As they accommodate to society, they accommodate to one another. And we should expect that as disintegration takes place, human relations would grow more disruptive.

In a period of religious integration, for instance, men are fellow-worshippers, allies in a relationship to a deity or a religious institution. This does not say anything about what their relationship toward one another ought to be, but they are all aboard the same boat, and they develop favorable attitudes toward one another insofar as they reinforce one another's beliefs.

In such a period too, we expect to find the family as the basic religious unit. But the relation between the family extends further, to the village, to all men who become familiar in the life of an individual. The "familial" relationship can be said to be prevalent among men; agreements are kept, obligations are met because men would not think of doing anything else.

The relationships are essentially unconscious. Men do what they are expected to do and think as they are expected to think, because alternative possibilities do not present themselves. When someone does behave in unexpected ways, his violation of the codes is regarded as utterly shocking.

But time passes and the civilization elaborates and develops. Social interaction increases and men must deal more frequently with strangers. Social and economic interaction becomes more impersonal and pragmatic. You make an exchange for your own benefit. The stranger must look out for himself and you must look out for yourself. Or, to insure that he lives up to his end of the bargain, you bind him to a contract. And so relations grow more impersonal, and men are less and less aware of many of the consequences of their acts. As the scope of a culture widens, men travel more, lose their relations to the land and family from which they came, fall back more on their own resources in a world that is much less secure, and become more guarded, more selfish, more cynical.

Eventually, if the process carries far enough and reconstitution is not effected, some men become ruthless, determined to gain their own political and economic ends regardless of the costs others may have to pay. Such conduct will not go unnoticed, will be criticized, regarded as immoral, even punished. A growing concern about immorality will manifest itself as people become aware that more and more people are deviating from the old standards. There will be attempts to reassert the existing standards, which are likely to be unsuccessful, and there will be attempts to readjust the standards to changing conditions, a call for the transvaluation of values, which may be part of a successful reconstitution.

But if a new set of standards cannot be established — and this is very difficult — continued adherence to the old will be increasingly regarded as hypocritical or naive. Ruthlessness, characterized by full exploitation of advantages, will manifest itself in new aspects. Ruthlessness is the logical consequence of rational pragmatism. The concept of mercy has no relevance: it might be foolish, because any weakness might give opportunity for a ruthless response.

Demagogues, potential Caesars, appear. The will to power, however masked by doctrines and ideologies, underlies effective political action. The Caesar will be supported by some who worship him as a manifestation of their own unreachable desires, and by some who hope to gain power, prestige or wealth by his triumph. He may be an effective ruler, but his primary purpose is to maintain his personal power. The type is also exemplified by the Greek tyrants, and upstarts like Liu Pang or Napoleon.

As ruthlessness reaches new heights, as barbarous conduct manifests itself uninhibited by old codes of morality or any sense of purpose beyond individual gain, callousness will become increasingly prevalent. People will turn away from abuses to a system they no longer respect, and from fellow men they do not know and do not care about. What callousness involves, above all, is a repression of the feelings and emotions associated with land/family phases of civilization. Relationships among persons take a long time to grow. The nomadic megalopolitan constantly acquires different neighbors, and even though he may profess great friendship for them, that friendship must of necessity be artificial. The neighbor is a device to provide support and security, and when the nomad moves again, he must seek a similar device, as he seeks a similar house and the food to which he is accustomed. Naturally he will sacrifice any one of these individuals so long as they are available as types. Thus he will not lift a finger to support his neighbor, he will deliberately avoid becoming "involved" in order to save himself the pangs of separation.

Impersonality is sometimes enforced by technological distance. One's own acts of ruthlessness are not personally experienced; they become merely decisions that have to be made. This technological advantage is particularly soothing to Faustian man. In war he does not usually see the enemy he kills; even in civil life claims of property or other grievances are settled between representatives of the aggrieved parties on an impersonal basis. The push-button nuclear rocket is the ultimate in the impersonal approach to social change.

But where such convenient protections are lacking, defenses can be developed. Exposure to suffering, even one's own, leads to a diminishing response. It is simply impossible to reach repeated levels of concern and empathy. The wider spread the suffering, the easier it is to endure. And eventually the suffering becomes institutionalized. Games of death are conducted under certain rules; the storming of a city leads to certain ends previously understood and accepted; revolutionary tribunals are organized to expedite the destructive process; victims in a prison camp are executed en masse, lacking even the dignity of individual identification.

Suffering will increase from conflict, from anarchy, from senseless and arbitrary use of force, from loneliness, from every day lack of consideration. In a thousand ways, great and small, men will inflict pain and humiliation on one another while those not affected look on, or look away, or look on but don't see. Those who inflict suffering do so because they don't care, because they are too far removed from the suffering they cause, or because they find meaning in the suffering, they like to inflict it.

Ultimately this process must reach a point beyond which it cannot go. Callousness ceases when the observers become the victims, and then there must either be a reaction of counter-ruthlessness, such as peasants' revolutions, or a general weariness with regard to the whole process, and a deep desire for a return to order, for peace at any price. Leaders who manifest confidence and show a penchant for simplification command surprising support if they look like restoring order to human relationships. Callousness is replaced by a reaction against ruthlessness and inhumanity, a conscious re-examination of feelings and a search for those aspects of a culture that seem to reaffirm the brotherhood of man. Whereas brotherhood had once existed unconsciously under an established order, now it becomes something that has to be thought about and felt for.

Unless a civilization returns to a feudal state, however, there can never be a return to the unconscious, familiar relationship first described. The complexity of states and empires require, the maintenance of contractural relationships. Nor can the lack of self-consciousness, characteristic of periods of origin, be regained in periods of revival.

NOTES

a. The Will to Power

I have suggested in the last two chapters that the will to power appears most strongly in periods of transition. A Toynbean dominant minority seizes power regretfully until it is replaced by a Spenglerian Caesar who delights in it. There is an increasing tendency, in other words, for men to become interested in power for its own sake as other standards of value cease to have meaning.

But this is not to say that power considerations do not play a role in more integrated periods. If something is going to run, somebody has to run it, and whoever does usually is there because he wants to be. Where the will to power is not an important factor in the culture spectrum, the culture is not going to be politically significant, and if it is not politically significant it is not likely to be a great culture. And generally, regardless of the trappings, things work best under a strong leader who knows how to use the mechanisms of power that have fallen to him.

b. Weariness vs. Universalism

The view expressed in the previous two sections that some kind of social weariness is a prerequisite to any kind of political unification seems rather negative in a world in which people are getting thrown in jail for advocating world peace and the universal brotherhood of man. But militant pacifism is the response of a small minority that is temperamentally fit for it. The more common response is either to fight back or to give up. In a sense giving up sets the stage for a successful transition. Finding virtues in a former enemy is a solace for defeat. The brotherhood of man, and most of its variations, if achieved, turns out in the last analysis to be a rationalization, not a commitment.

c. Abdication of Local Pride

One of the political consequences of rootlessness seems to be an abdication of local pride and loyalty. As people move from one place to another, they take less interest in how any particular locality is governed. They will move on again anyhow. This leaves local government to those who are going to stay, almost by definition the less successful. When roads must be built, rivers cleaned, schools constructed, central government is compelled to move in or nothing will happen.

4: ATTITUDES TOWARD FORM

There is a hill above the town of Hastings, England. As you look to the right you can see the old part of town, bending in upon itself, a pleasing mixture of white and brown, comfortable, delightful. To the left you can see the new part of town with its red bricks, its straight roads, its industry and efficiency. The two parts of town look so strikingly different that it is hard to believe there can be any relation between them. Europe is full of towns divided in this way and we go from the new towns, that represent our way of life, to see the old, to try to recapture what it was that we have lost. But if we want to recapture it, we had better look from afar. If we go into the old town we shall observe the television antennae, the grandmother making out her football pools while the baby gnaws a chocolate smelling plastic puzzle approved by Ph.D's. The old town is only a shell that recalls another life, another set of attitudes.

What the old towns and villages had, and the planned new towns singularly lack, was a sense of form. Why? Was it because the building materials were of the surrounding country or because the need for protection established the boundaries of what was to be defended? Or was it because the culture was so well integrated that the form had to be there without anyone thinking about it. Looking at the sudden departure of the new city from the old town, it is hard to escape the impression that external structure very accurately represents internal attitude. And the recurrent process of urbanization, in which individually planned structures and spaces combine in a total and incomplete formlessness, is simply a graphic physical example of the process of transition from one form of integration to another. External structures do reflect the inner sense of form or the lack of it. Aesthetic indicators — the architecture, sculpture, painting of a culture — very accurately reflect the development of ideas and feelings of the time.

An agrarian culture usually has a built-in sense of proportion. Artifacts are constructed because they have a basic, functional relationship to the culture. A farm house contains what is needed for living, a church what is needed for worship. The use of local materials is very natural, of course, and it reinforces in turn the naturalness of the situation.

But as a culture continues to develop there comes a time when artificial choices begin to present themselves. Families have enough in housing, furniture and equipment to suit their immediate needs. Now they can choose to try to raise standards of living or make non-functional creations, to whittle or carve or paint. And there is a tendency as time goes by for elaboration to take place, for creative tendencies to progress from the simple to the ornate as they progress from the unconscious to the conscious. Consciousness of form does not mean that deterioration is taking place. Whether one prefers a Gothic cathedral to one by Wren or a provincial village to an eighteenth-century crescent is largely a matter of taste or mood within an individual. The development of consciousness is accompanied by sets of established standards and praise is earned for success in interpreting these standards. Men come to think of themselves as architects rather than builders, they are conscious of creative capacity, of the ability to interpret standards in fresh and original ways.

But ultimately the prevailing forms of a culture are fully developed. Men now face a growing dilemma that pervades their lives. Just as the old standards no longer apply in politics or economics or attitudes toward society, the old standards of form no longer are appropriate. Elaboration becomes excessive and finally ridiculous. In order to avoid repetition the builder or the writer tends toward extremes of size, color or gawdiness. In the search for effect, styles are randomly borrowed and combined, and the sense of proportion is lost. Ramessid colossalism or Rococo elaboration are the result of impulses of this kind.

The loss of proportion reflects the dissolution of the old forms. But just as the forms of an integrated culture tend to be pervasive, we should expect formlessness to become increasingly pervasive as the process of disintegration continues. The formlessness will be reflected in the deterioration of physical forms representing a transition in attitudes. The process is neither good nor bad in itself, for without the breaking down of old forms, there can be no reconstitution.

Just as the rooted family of the integrated agrarian culture had a built-in sense of form, the loss of roots contributes in many ways to formlessness. The loss of traditions, the weakening of the family structure, cosmopolitanism, the development of transportation and communications all act against distinguishing separation, stability and order. All serve to blend cultural individuality, to create a universal whole lacking the separate resources for further creation. Standardization and uniformity are essential to the urban nomad since he finds security in having the same kinds of people and things about him wherever he may happen to be. So there emerges a mish-mash culture characterized by interchangeable people. The universal cosmopolitan type is consistent with a formless culture.

Just as the Hastings village manifests a form that no longer has substance, so other formal relics survive. The institutions of government will be retained by a Caesar who rules because these institutions have no meaning. The church retains its form of service, but it conveys nothing to the dwindling congregations. The flag symbolizes the nation, but people are weary with what the nation stands for, children are bored by ceremonies, soldiers serve because they must.

Much energy in a mature culture is devoted to fighting formless tendencies. City planners fight to make external sense out of internal nonsense. Industries have organization charts, generals have maps for battles they cannot see, the businessman hires secretaries to keep files intended to make sense of what he is doing. One of the most commonly used devices to standardize and order both the commercial and the governmental world is very appropriately called a "form," and there are hundreds of jokes, themselves rather standardized, on how these forms fail to fulfill their purpose and add to the chaos in triplicate.

If reconstitution is going to take place, new forms will eventually replace those that have broken down. While critics deplore the loss of standards, some artists may sense glimmerings of something new, something relevant to the problems of their time. But in a world conditioned only by the old, it is difficult to distinguish between what represents a genuinely successful discovery of forms appropriate to the coming integration and what are simply desperate and meaningless and blind experiments. Or, it may not be the artist, but the engineer or the craftsman, seeking to solve problems of his time, who develops the appropriate forms. But consciousness once discovered cannot be lost again. Any reconstitution that does not return to feudalism will have to accept a conscious relationship of forms and attitudes.

Formlessness underlies the attitudes of disintegration. It is the pervading factor. Its predominance negates the study of form. Someone who wants to understand such a culture will miss the point if he concentrates on the government, the economic system, the manners and the religion. These may be empty shells. He cannot understand an international system by studying trade agreements or diplomatic negotiations or battles or lists of land areas won and lost. But this is not to say that pervasive formlessness is to be equated with universal meaninglessness. Just because what happens may be meaningless, the struggle to find meaning is of particular relevance. The world of ideas and attitudes is the world that matters here. You cannot understand the physical form without understanding what is happening in the intellectual and emotional underground.

We have seen that in periods of integration most of the attitudes in a culture will have to do with preserving or modifying that culture and the people and forms that compose it. In times of transition the fabric and ideas of the culture will come under attack, many will be destroyed, but there will also be attitudes and forces working toward a new kind of synthesis.

It now remains to incorporate the physical and psychic indicators of cultural phase into the basic model of a civilization.

NOTES

a. The Meaning of Originality

Ordinarily we associate originality with the process of growth. But when men value originality for its own sake, when they strive to be original, when they guard their ideas for fear that others might receive credit for them, then we might suspect that a pattern is nearing the end of its development. The consciousness of originality may then mean that there is not much left in the pattern to develop, or that men seek to escape the pattern. When a style is in the process of development there is so much to be done and the supply is so plentiful that one need not worry about protecting one's ideas.

b. Criticism, Classification, Codification

Another sign that a pattern has reached its culmination is the tendency for men to step back and look at it. They criticize contemporary development against standards for the whole; they classify discoveries and discoverers and group men into schools according to their differences and similarities; they codify laws, manners, customs; there is a great deal of summarization in the air.

c. The Problem of Transitional Creation

The talented artist or writer faces a difficult problem in periods of transition. He cannot follow the old patterns because they have been worked out. His efforts to establish new ones depend on his intuitive understanding of his own times and his luck in feeling for the future. He will be harshly criticized by the establishment, which supports the old standards long after they become obsolescent. He will compete with a large number of frauds, since it is difficult for anyone to criticize that for which no standards are established. Thus the painter may have to compete with apes or infants who slosh at random and may hit on some satisfying combinations. The pioneer of new patterns can hope for little recognition even if he successfully establishes a pattern for the future. Who painted before Giotto anyway? And it is likely that however well he conceives his patterns, they will in the end not be adopted. Like a talented sperm cell, he will probably miss the egg. In the face of these odds the transitional artist must possess unusual self-confidence, or what in another age would have been called faith. He can maintain himself only if his goal is something far greater than recognition.

d. Comparative Historians as Interpreters of Art

The comparative historians are probably unreliable in their interpretations of abstract art. They tend to associate abstractness with formless and representation with form. Yet abstraction is often concerned with pure form — witness cubism — while representation often indicates a dissolution of form — consider impressionism. Do new forms emerge from abstractionism? Or is abstraction the Faustian method of pursuing the limitless unknown?

The problem of the historian judging the artist may be illustrated by a story about Flinders Petrie. Petrie's provocative little book, *The Revolutions of Civilisation* is full of pictures illustrating "archaic," "developed" and "decadent" sculpture and panting in various civilizations. R. G. Collingwood clipped the pictures from Petrie's book and showed them to various artists, asking which were archaic and which were decadent. To Collingwood's delight, the artists in many instances identified Petrie's "decadent" pictures as being superior art to those Petrie thought represented the culmination of a civilization's achievement.

When Petrie learned about this he remarked that it only showed how decadent the artists of his own time had become.

e. Colossalism

Toynbee uses the term to describe excesses of size which appear when quantity replaces quality, when a creative pattern can bear no more elaboration and must be treated with greater exaggeration if something different is to bee produced. Thus the Pharaohs strove to build pyramids that were bigger than those of their predecessors, builders of sky scrapers race each other to see who can go the highest. Toynbee says nothing, as far as I know, about twelve-volume studies of history.

f. Archaism and Futurism

The terms archaism and futurism are used by Toynbee and others to describe conscious efforts to deal with the problem of formlessness. The conscious desire to return to a period in the past that seemed better or to destroy the present and create something new on the spot are likely to fail because they do not come from any inner inspiration but from the desperate feeling that anything is better than the existing condition.

On the other hand, solutions to problems may involve what appears to be archaism. A painter, for instance, may borrow forms from the past, consciously or unconsciously, because they have relevance to the problem he is dealing with. Or he may invent something — not because he set out to do something new at all costs — but because in dealing with his problem something new came out of him.

The form and the action, then, are not enough. We have also to understand the circumstances, the motivations, the attitudes that underlie the form and the action. Archaism and futurism ar useful concepts in generalizing about kinds of reactions to formlessness. But they are dangerous if used as all-encompassing categories.

Sources

A. Attitudes Toward the World

Theories of material/spiritual dichotomies are elaborately developed by both Arnold Toynbee and Pitirim Sorokin: *A Study of History*, VII: 381-568, "Universal Churches" and *Social and Cultural Dynamics*, abridged ed., Part One, 2-66, respectively. See also Toynbee, *Study*, V: 376-82, 557-9, "Alternative Behavior and Feeling"; Sorokin, *Society, Culture and Personality*, Chapter 41, pp. 607-19; Nikolai Berdyaev, *The Meaning of History*, pp. 210-19; Albert Schweitzer, *The Decay and The Restoration of Civilization*, Chapter 2, "Hindrances in Spiritual Life"; Philip Bagby, *Culture and History*, pp. 206-15.

B. Attitudes Toward Society

Most relevant on the relationship between attitudes, aesthetic vitality and social-political forms are Oswald Spengler, *The Decline of The West*, II: 169-84, National Character; Toynbee, *A Study of History*, III: 337-390, "Differentiation through Growth"; IV: 303-20; Sorokin, *Social and Cultural Dynamics*, III: 364-75; A. L. Kroeber, *Style and Civilizations*, pp. 137-49, "The Art Approach to Civilizations"; Christopher Dawson, *Dynamics of World History*, pp. 68-74, "Art and Society"; Flinders Petrie, *The Revolutions of Civilisation* — the entire book is built on the aesthetic approach; Jacob Burckhardt, *Force and Freedom*, pp. 169-184, "Culture Determined by the State" and pp. 211-230, "The State Determined by Culture."

C. Attitudes Toward Man

Familar and contractual relationships: Sorokin, *Social and Cultural Dynamics*, abridged ed., pp. 445-9. Power struggles: Spengler, *The Decline of The West*, II: 431-35; Toynbee, *A Study of History*, V: 35-58. Ruthlessness and callousness: Spengler, *Decline*, II: 420-35; Sorokin, *Society, Culture and Personality*, pp. 617-9; Toynbee, *Civilization on Trial*, pp. 161-3. Weariness and universalism: Spengler, *Decline*, II: 184-6, 432-5; Sorokin, *Dynamics*, IV: 777; Toynbee, *Study*, V: 342-3, VII: 69-80, VI: 1-48.

D. ATTITUDES TOWARD FORM

Mass formlessness: Toynbee, *A Study of History*, V: 439-569; Christopher Dawson, *The Dynamics of World History*, pp. 54-67; Philip Bagby, *Culture and History*, pp. 212-6; Berdyaev, *The Meaning of History*, pp. 209-12. Urban formlessness: Spengler *The Decline of The West*, II: 85-110; I: 31-3; A. L. Kroeber, *Anthropology*, 280-6. Aesthetic form and formlessness: Spengler, *Decline*, I: 217-96; Toynbee, *Study*, V: 480-3; Kroeber, *Style and Civilizations*, pp. 137-49; Sorokin, *Social and Cultural Dynamics*, abridged ed., pp. 68-224; Flinders Petrie, *The Revolutions of Civilisation*. Other indicators of formlessness: Toynbee, *Study*, III: 153-54; V: 383-84; VI: 51-63; Sorokin, *Dynamics*, abridged ed., pp. 170-1.

V

A MODEL OF DEVELOPMENT

1: Charting the Model

In this chapter I shall offer a model of a civilization that is derived from the material presented in the preceding chapters.

Earlier we derived a basic model that took into consideration all possibilities of disintegration, ossification and reconstitution and left open, therefore, an infinite number of possible combinations. But since disintegration and ossification spell the end of a particular system, we do not need to know what will occur beyond them. Reconstitution represents a repeat of a situation that has already occurred, and therefore part of the model is simply used again. To include the repeats in the model would be like writing out repeated music a second time. What remains, then, is a progression of phases from the feudal through the imperial system. And even here, partly for the sake of manageability and partly because of ignorance, I should like to omit the initial and final transitional phases. That leaves a sequence from a crystalized feudal system through a crystalized imperial system:

FC - FT - SC - ST - IC

The model is probably still too much oriented to the West, for Spengler, Toynbee and Sorokin all draw more on European, Mediterranean and western Asian examples. I have not attempted to illustrate each of the many generalizations included here. To do so I would have had to dig out many examples not used by the comparative historians themselves, and this would have made a different model. Besides, the model is already too busy, too inclusive; it is in need of simplification, not complication.

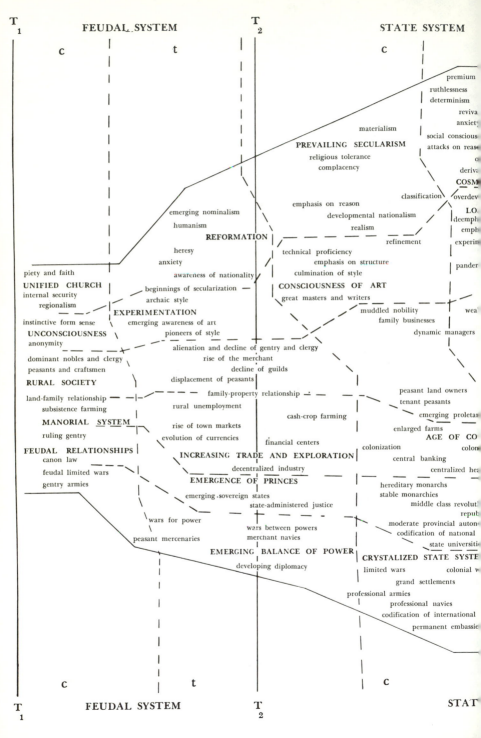

FEUDAL SYSTEM

T₁ · c · t · T₂ · c · STATE SYSTEM

premium
ruthlessness
determinism
reviva
anxiet
social conscious
attacks on reas
o
deriv

materialism

PREVAILING SECULARISM
religious tolerance
complacency

COSM

classification overdev

emphasis on reason
developmental nationalism
realism

L.O.
deemph
emph
experin

emerging nominalism
humanism

REFORMATION

refinement

pander

heresy
anxiety
awareness of nationality

technical proficiency
emphasis on structure
culmination of style

piety and faith
UNIFIED CHURCH
internal security
regionalism

beginnings of secularization —
archaic style

CONSCIOUSNESS OF ART
great masters and writers

muddled nobility
family businesses

wea

instinctive form sense
UNCONSCIOUSNESS
anonymity

EXPERIMENTATION
emerging awareness of art
pioneers of style

dynamic managers

alienation and decline of gentry and clergy
rise of the merchant
decline of guilds
displacement of peasants

dominant nobles and clergy
peasants and craftsmen
RURAL SOCIETY

land-family relationship —
subsistence farming
MANORIAL SYSTEM
ruling gentry

family-property relationship ⁚ —
rural unemployment

peasant land owners
tenant peasants
emerging proleta

cash-crop farming

enlarged farms
AGE OF CO
colon

rise of town markets
evolution of currencies

financial centers

colonization
central banking
centralized hea

FEUDAL RELATIONSHIPS
canon law
feudal limited wars
gentry armies

INCREASING TRADE AND EXPLORATION
decentralized industry
EMERGENCE OF PRINCES
emerging sovereign states
state-administered justice

hereditary monarchs
stable monarchies
middle class revolut
repub

wars for power

peasant mercenaries

wars between powers
merchant navies
EMERGING BALANCE OF POWER
developing diplomacy

moderate provincial auton
codification of national
state universiti
CRYSTALIZED STATE SYSTE
limited wars   colonial v
grand settlements
professional armies
professional navies
codification of international
permanent embassie

T₁ · c · t · T₂ · c ·

FEUDAL SYSTEM

T₁   T₂   STAT

F

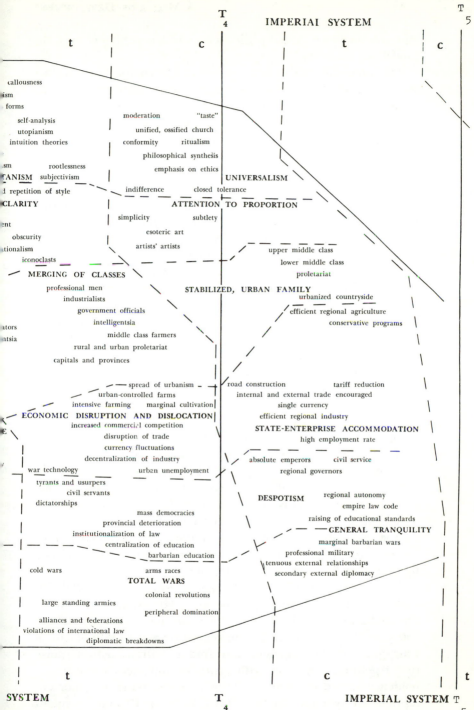

IMPERIAL SYSTEM

T4   T5

t   c   t   c

callousness
ism
forms
   self-analysis   moderation   "taste"
   utopianism   unified, ossified church
   intuition theories   conformity   ritualism
               philosophical synthesis
sm   rootlessness   emphasis on ethics
ANISM subjectivism   UNIVERSALISM
d repetition of style   indifference   closed tolerance
CLARITY   ATTENTION TO PROPORTION
ent   simplicity   subtlety
  obscurity   esoteric art
ationalism   artists' artists   upper middle class
  iconoclasts   lower middle class
  MERGING OF CLASSES   proletariat
   professional men
    industrialists   STABILIZED, URBAN FAMILY
      government officials   urbanized countryside
       intelligentsia   efficient regional agriculture
ators   middle class farmers   conservative programs
ntsia   rural and urban proletariat
    capitals and provinces

       spread of urbanism   road construction   tariff reduction
      urban-controlled farms   internal and external trade encouraged
   intensive farming   marginal cultivation   single currency
ECONOMIC DISRUPTION AND DISLOCATION   efficient regional industry
    increased commercial competition   STATE-ENTERPRISE ACCOMMODATION
E   disruption of trade   high employment rate
       currency fluctuations
     decentralization of industry   absolute emperors   civil service
y war technology   urban unemployment   regional governors
  tyrants and usurpers
    civil servants   DESPOTISM   regional autonomy
  dictatorships   empire law code
       mass democracies   raising of educational standards
    provincial deterioration   GENERAL TRANQUILITY
  institutionalization of law   marginal barbarian wars
    centralization of education   professional military
        barbarian education   tenuous external relationships
  cold wars   arms races   secondary external diplomacy
      TOTAL WARS
       colonial revolutions
  large standing armies
        peripheral domination
  alliances and federations
violations of international law
    diplomatic breakdowns

t   c   t

SYSTEM   T4   IMPERIAL SYSTEM T5

But the direction of simplification would depend on how the model was to be used.

The point is that it is better to tackle comparative history with a model that is in some respects inadequate than to read comparative history without any model at all. Without a frame of reference, it would be nearly impossible to absorb so much information, nor would there be any way of knowing what information could probably be set aside.

This is intended to be a working model, one that should be considerably modified when it is tested against several histories of civilizations. I look forward to doing some of the testing myself, but I hope the model may be of use to other students of history, philosophy and anthropology.

Putting this model into a diagram (Figure 5) has been a disconcerting experience. Such a diagram forms its own internal patterns, it seems to take on a life of its own. When it is finished, you have an uneasy feeling that it has departed considerably from the model it is supposed to illustrate. It would perhaps be more candid to say, as they do of movies derived from novels, that the diagram is *based* on the model.

The dotted horizontal lines separate the components of a civilization into six different categories. These, from top to bottom, are: outlook (Quigley's term, incorporating religion, philosophy and world view), aesthetics, society, economics, government, international relations. The solid horizontalish lines at top and bottom serve no other purpose than to reassure the diagram maker that his subject needn't have fuzzy edges.

The dotted lines that slant downward and to the left roughly separate alternate transitional and crystalized phases (indicated by t's and c's). The areas between these lines slant to the left on the assumption that psychic indicators tend to precede physical indicators (although they are in turn reshaped and modified by economic and political developments).

By contrast the solid, evenly spaced, vertical lines (labeled with T's) mark off equal time periods. For example, for Western civilization call T3 1750 and let the spaces represent about 250 years. Each vertical T line represents a sample moment of time, and any such moment may find a civilization in a transitional political stage but with attitudes and ideas indicating a tendency toward integration. Thus a person living at a moment represented by a vertical line drawn between T3 and T4 might

CRYSTALLIZED FEUDAL SYSTEM

Spirit / Life / World	*Form / Subject / Media / Artists*	*Upper Class / Middle Class / Laboring Classes / Country / Cities*	*Agriculture / Commerce / Finance / Industry*	*Rulers / Forms / Education*	*Peace / War / Forms / Rules*
Spirit piety faith unified church man glorifies God *Life* internal security external fear theological dogma *World* regionalism imperviousness	*Form* instinctive sense serves religious purpose *Subject* religious rural stylized type *Media* public structures folk songs verbal epics *Artists* amateur anonymous unconsciousness of art	*Upper Class* dominant nobles & churchmen family-land relationship monastic scholars *Middle Class* scattered townsmen organized craftsmen *Laboring Classes* peasant-based economy enlarged family *Country* rural society villages predominate few walled towns *Cities* rare and provincial	*Agriculture* subsistence farming manorial relationship *Commerce* itinerant traders *Finance* barter *Industry* manor crafts	*Rulers* lords church hierarchy *Forms* feudal relationships independent towns canon law *Education* church dominated monastic scholars	*Peace* seasonal religious *War* barbarian invasions feudal limited wars sieges gentry armies cavalry *Forms* feudalism *Rules* feudal obligations

FEUDAL SYSTEM IN TRANSITION

Spirit / Life / World	*Form / Subject / Media / Artists*	*Upper Class / Middle Class / Laboring Classes / Country / Cities*	*Agriculture / Commerce / Finance / Industry*	*Rulers / Forms / Education*	*Peace / War / Forms / Rules*
Spirit increasing nominalism reformation humanism God glorifies man *Life* anxiety theological philosophy heresy *World* militant provincialism national awareness new ideas welcomed	*Form* archaic style experimentation *Subject* secularization exoticism idealized type *Media* chants love poems epics *Artists* pioneers of style consciousness of art	*Upper Class* state confiscation heretical challenges alienation of priests superfluous gentry *Middle Class* decline of guild rise of merchant family-property relationship *Laboring Classes* imposed serfdom displacement of peasants migration to towns *Country* town market centers towns subordinate to states *Cities* incorporation of city states emergence of capital cities	*Agriculture* subsistence farming cash-crop farming state-controlled land private estates town markets rural unemployment *Commerce* increasing trade exploration *Finance* major currencies accumulating capital *Industry* declining crafts decentralized industry specialization indirect production	*Rulers* tyrants' revolutions emergence of princes councils of nobles *Forms* secularizing aristocracies emerging sovereign states canon law challengd state justice *Education* private, secular tutors apprenticeships	*Peace* exhaustion peaces *War* wars for power wars between powers religious wars external economic wars gentry armies peasant mercenaries horse and foot armies merchant navies *Forms* expanding states states limiting states incorporation of city states *Rules* law by custom developing diplomacy

Figure 6

PHASE	OUTLOOK	AESTHETICS	SOCIETY	ECONOMICS	GOVERNMENT	INTERNATIONAL
CRYSTALLIZED **STATE** **SYSTEM**	*Spirit* pragmatism materialism secularization church/state separation religious tolerance man glorifies man *Life* complacency self-consciousness realism emphasis on reason basic scientific concepts classification *World* developmental nationalism closed tolerance	*Form* culmination of style technical proficiency elaboration refinement emphasis on musical structure, poetic form *Subject* realism social consciousness social representatives unique secondary characters *Media* secular music secular plays essays prose novels interior decorating *Artists* great masters and writers consciousness of form individual style sought	*Upper Class* distinguished nobility purchased nobility provincial nobility *Middle Class* wealthy parvenus dynamic business leaders family businesses professional administrators intelligentsia peasant land owners *Laboring Classes* tenant peasants break-up of enlarged family emerging proletariat *Country* backwater villages age of towns rising population *Cities* capital cities seaports commerce centers	*Agriculture* cash-crop farming enlarged farms new farm methods *Commerce* age of commerce colonization colonial trade *Finance* central banking capital investment *Industry* centralized industry government-supported industry heavy industry standardization innovation urban employment	*Rulers* hereditary monarch rise of middle-class ministers *Forms* stable monarchies moderate provincial autonomy middle class republics revolutions professional administration codification of national law *Education* universities vocational education private schools	*Peace* truces grand settlements *War* limited wars colonial wars professional armies wartime citizen armies professional navies *Forms* balance of power systems of alliance *Rules* codification of international law elaborate codes of diplomacy permanent embassies
STATE **SYSTEM** **IN** **TRANSITION**	*Spirit* premium of comfort extreme pragmatism ruthlessness callousness stoicism determinism revival of religious forms search for universal truth man denounces man	*Form* overdevelopment repetition loss of clarity form deemphasized content emphasized colossalism experimentation obscurity revivals	*Middle Class* merging of classes middle class farmers professional men industrialists government officials professional military demagogues intelligentsia	*Agriculture* urban-controlled farms big farms intensive farming marginal cultivation soil exhaustion sporadic subsistence farming migration to cities *Commerce* increased competition war interrupts trade trade balance problems tariffs	*Rulers* caesars civil servants managers *Forms* tyrannies dictatorships mass democracy provincial decline bureaucracy institutionalization of law	*Peace* cold wars arms races exhaustion peaces *War* total wars colonial revolutions guerrilla warfare large standing armies rotating conscription

Figure 6 (contd.)

STATE SYSTEM IN TRANSITION (contd.)

anxiety
individualism
self-analysis
social conscience
weariness
compartmentalization
utopianism
attacks on reason
intuition theories
nature theories
classification

World
derivative
nationalism
rootlessness
cosmopolitanism
open tolerance
alien values perceived

Subject
fantasy
erotica
subjectivism
sensationalism
internal exploration

Media
formless novel
free verse
improvised music
rhythm explorations
proliferation of media

Artists
iconoclasts
panderers
migration to cities

Laboring Classes
rural proletariat
urban proletariat

Country
"hick" towns
tourist towns
provincial cities

Cities
cynosures
spread of urbanism
cosmopolitanism
family disintegration
rising population

cartels
colonial competition

Finance
inflation
price fixing
currency fluctuations

Industry
war technology
production of luxury goods
decentralization of industry
decline in basic production
industrial collusion
urban unemployment

Education
institutionalization
central control
mass education
barbarian education

Forms
threats to balance
peripheral domination
attempted federations

Rules
violations of law
diplomatic breakdowns

CRYSTALLIZED IMPERIAL SYSTEM

Spirit
moderation
modest living
"taste"
religious mergers
unified, ossified church
cultural perspective
man accepts man

Life
conformity
ritualism
passiveness
philosophical synthesis
philosophical pragmatism
sanding and polishing
emphasis on ethics

World
universalism
indifference
closed tolerance

Form
attention to proportion
esoteric art
quiet art
simplicity

Subject
mundane
inoffensive
subtle delineation

Media
polished prose
incidental music
orthodox materials

Artists
artists' artists
absence of genius
contempt for individual style

Middle Class
upper middle class
lower middle class
respectable people

Laboring Classes
proletariat
stabilized family

Country
artificial countryside
vacations

Cities
greater urban areas
urbanized countryside
urban family
population leveling

Agriculture
efficient regional agriculture
conservation
rural poverty reduced

Commerce
road construction
tariffs eliminated
internal trade encouraged
trade with other civilizations
trade with barbarians

Finance
single currency

Industry
efficient regional industry
state enterprise
accommodation
high employment rate

Rulers
absolute emperor
civil servants
regional governors
provincial managers

Forms
despotism
centralized rule
regional autonomy
administrative reform
empire law code

Education
extension of higher education
raising of "standards"
reduction of mass education

Peace
marginal barbarian

War
internal power wars
marginal barbarian wars
limited civilizational wars
professional soldiers
small mobile armies

Forms
centralized government
tenuous external relationships

Rules
empire law code
secondary external diplomacy

Figure 6 (contd.)

see a state system around him but feel empire in the air. The diagram shows, therefore, that the transformation from state system to empire cannot be designated by anything like the date of a battle.

The diagram shows to some extent the increases and decreases in importance of various components that make up a civilization. We have no terms with which to measure the relative importance of cash-crop farming and archaic sculpture, of course, but the total impression conveyed is one of a swelling of activities in the period of the state system and the beginnings of contraction at the onset of empire.

Figure 6 portrays the civilization with still greater distortion but also with greater order (an example of striving against the odds for form?). Preliminary indications are that despite its possible inferiority to the diagram in aesthetic interest, this table is more useful for a research model, while the diagram has been more interesting as a teaching device. A researcher might use such a table (elaborating and substituting more relevant categories) as a frame of reference for comparative study.

NOTES

a. "Infinite" Combinations

When I say that the model of a civilization shows an infinite number of possible combinations, I mean that there would be no end to the ways in which phases of civilizations could be fitted together or to the length of time a civilization could theoretically exist. But this does not mean that at any given time any phase can follow any other or that there are an infinite number of kinds of phases. A finite number of elements can relate to one another in an infinite number of ways, but not all of these elements can relate to all others.

b. The Direction of Time

In the diagram time flows from left to right (because Western writing flows that way), in the table it drops from top to bottom. Which way does time flow in the West? Hour glasses go from top to bottom, calendars read from left to right and clocks go round and round. I asked an international relations class and the students were evenly divided between horizontal and vertical (though all agreed that it does not flow from bottom to top or right to left).

Only one student thought the question ridiculous.

2: THE FEUDAL SYSTEM

A feudal system comes into existence as the first step beyond a nomadic or other subsistence culture, or when it is recovering from a major disaster, as in the case of China after the fall of the Han empire. In times of disaster or rapid transition, people fend for themselves as best they can. They look for protection to whomever is near to give it, and they rely on themselves to produce their own food and shelter.

When the disaster is over, what emerges is a system in which subsistence farming predominates; in which complex economic arrangements exist between those who do the farming — peasants — and their political overlords; in which these overlords in turn have intricately ramified political relationships with one another; and in which some kind of ritualized religious synthesis prevails.

Since lines of central authority for a large political area do not exist, the feudal relationship is one of extreme complexity. Each member of the gentry must establish relationships with each other member with whom he comes in contact. And these relationships become bent and changed and encumbered as prestige and tradition are challenged by fluctuations in power. People living in a feudal system are almost unaware of overall relationships, and ordinarily powers at one end will have little to do with powers at the other. But these powers, and those in between, will seem to the historian to behave in a similar manner, to be coming up with similar solutions to similar problems.

Feudal wars will be largely wars of power and prestige, since there will be few ideological differences and wealth will tend to be used more for increasing prestige than for raising overall living standards. These wars will be limited, fought at convenient times of the year by gentry armies, the peasants and townspeople more often inconvenienced and annoyed than injured or obliterated. Campaigns last only a season, not for decades. A peasant may lose his crop to an army, may be killed or starve to death, but the peasantry goes on planting and harvesting and reproducing. Towns may be under siege, but most of them are not, and only rarely is one taken, and when it is it may ransom itself, or at worst lose its freedom, but not its existence. Warfare has a place in feudal cultures; it does not dominate them.

Religion has played a major role in the transition that preceded the crystalized feudal society. It gave a style that made possible a wider range of identification, and it provided a fervor that enabled men to overcome obstacles in rebuilding. It is not surprising, therefore, that a dual government exists in most feudal cultures, though the proportions of the mixture may vary considerably. A spiritual structure exists, and men have obligations to their religion and the guidance of canon law. At the same time temporal problems are often taken to institutions provided by the nobility. It is the function of each member of the gentry to provide internal and external protection for those under his aegis.

Basically a feudal system relies on subsistence farming within a manorial relationship: the peasants produce food for themselves, for the gentry and for manor or village craftsmen who may be specializing in maintenance or production of artifacts. Even townsmen may help in the fields at certain times of the year. Exchange is most frequently made in kind, usually with itinerant traders bringing exotic goods from distant places. There is no point in trading with the peasant from the next village: he produces the same things you do.

Most people are peasants. Power is shared by the gentry and the clergy. Most craftsmen in the villages are indistinguishable from the peasants in their appearance and ways of thinking and feeling. But townsmen may take pride in feeling that they are above the peasants and different from and independent from the nobility. If there can be said to be a differentiated class of scholars, it is usually to be found within the clergy, except in China, where the gentry performed the clerical role.

The feudal society is essentially rural with a sprinkling of very small villages and an occasional larger one. Towns are relatively few, but differentiated from the village by outlook and often by a physical wall as well. The close-knit, enlarged family remains the basic unit in all classes. Three generations are likely to live on the same land, and close regional and emotional ties are likely to be maintained with siblings and other kin.

The feudal culture probably provides a maximum amount of security of a certain kind. Men are pious, they have faith in their religion. While this gives them a great deal of security against different kinds of fears, these fears are more numerous and more inexplicable than they may be in a more rational period. Philosophy and theology tend to be closely related in feudal periods. The theological dogma pervades everything else, controls it, limits it. Curiosity and the habit of inquiry are not likely to receive encouragement.

The aesthetic forms that exist are never thought of as art and usually, as a matter of fact, they are not very interesting. Anything that is constructed serves either a functional or a religious purpose. There is frequently clarity and simplicity in form, but the forms are likely to be repetitive, monotonous, conforming.

The feudal system is likely to have a minimum of relationships with outside cultures. The barbarian invasions of the formative period will have to be reduced or the civilization can never get started. The system, of course, may be overwhelmed by an older and physically superior system. If this happens, it will be wiped out, or incorporated in the larger system, and we shall study that instead. Or it may be cramped, but not destroyed, and then we shall get the anomalous development that Spengler calls "pseudomorphosis" (see note). Assuming such a disaster does not occur, the feudal state will probably be impervious to alien attitudes, ideas and aesthetics unless they are brought in by force. Feudal culture, though it lacks a political or economic center, is a closed, self-contained system.

NOTES

a. Pseudomorphosis

Spengler borrows the term from geologists, who use it to describe rocks that have developed irregular forms because of outside pressures. The term is appropriate to describe what happens to feudal cultures that are impeded in their development by strong neighbors. If this happens at the critical formative phase, we can expect that the subsequent development of the civilization will be unusual. Such a civilization must be distinguished from Toynbee's "abortive" civilizatons which were prevented from developing at all or "arrested" civilizations which were ossified at an early stage. The Middle East, that seeding-ground of civilizations, is probably the area that has produced the best examples of this phenomenon. (Pseudomorphosis is discussed in other contexts in Chapters VI, section 2 and VII, section 2.)

b. The Crusades

While wars of religion are to be expected in the marches of a feudal system, I should be surprised if centrally organized crusades turn out to be a recurrent phenomenon. These came about because of an awareness of the origin of the religion of Western civilization, bcause this area happened to be occupied by a more advanced civilization based on another religion, and because of the peculiar temperament and organizing power of the West.

3: THE WANING OF THE MIDDLE AGES

Civilizations differ from primitive cultures in their capacity for change. If a primitive culture is operating effectively, it is likely to maintain itself as it is for long periods. But when a civilization is operating effectively, it is likely to grow. Men will improve in their capacity to produce, and that in turn will be accompanied by more capital, more demand for markets, more leisure in which to produce ideas, a change in atmosphere, a tension on existing institutions that cease to be appropriate. As these institutions fail to meet the problems they were created to solve, they begin to break down, or their functions begin to be assumed by newer, more appropriate institutions.

The transition between a feudal and a state system is characterized by the disintegration of subsistence farming, the increasing importance of towns and their concommitant challenge to the political authority of the gentry, and the breakdown of the religious synthesis and dual government. In this situation, a new kind of political authority has been necessary, and monarchy seems to have been the form that usually emerges. In such a phase, dynamic, charismatic leaders have an unusual chance to expand their area of control, and the emergence of several such leaders over a relatively short period of time is not uncommon. Whether they establish governments that exert effective control over more distant regions depends on whether they are followed by politically astute consolidators. But sooner or later such a combination of leadership will emerge, and new types of states will begin to appear.

In such periods warfare is likely to be chronic. It will take place within the sovereign states, between the states, and with other civilizations. The civil wars continue until one sovereign establishes undisputed supremacy over a region. The interpower wars often arise out of a lack of clarification of territorial control, particularly when emerging dynasties have established scattered holdings through marriage. These wars will be more violent if they are accompanied by religious differences between the disputants, and intermittent periods of peace are more likely to come about from exhaustion than from mutual agreement. External wars are likely to take place in disputes over trading rights or where agents of merchants and traders come into contact with barbarians. If the religious aspects of the international struggle are carried to external areas, conflicts with barbarians are likely to be more savage and conflicts between representatives of different powers more ruthless.

Commerce, like warfare, develops between the incipient states, and greatly increases with territories outside the civilization. The crystalization of political units leads to the adoption of a few major currencies and the reduction of trade barriers.

The beginning of cash-crop agriculture leads to the creation of surplus labor, as well as goods, some of which is absorbed in trade — in the manning of vessels, for instance — and some of which is absorbed in town crafts and to a lesser extent in incipient, decentralized industry. The latter appears as increased population, and the demand of those no longer self-sufficient puts a strain on the productive capacities of craftsmen.

The town is the center of activity, serving as market center for the surrounding villages. Peasants bring surpluses from the manor to sell or trade. Members of the gentry frequent the towns seeking luxuries brought by merchants from distant lands. While the towns maintain their independence with relation to the surrounding nobility, they are gradually, by choice or compulsion, pledging allegiance to a prince. The latter can if need be command the weapons, resources and manpower necessary to conduct a successful siege.

The life of the peasant in this phase is likely to be less secure than it was in earlier times. He may be as well off economically, but there is more likely to be dissatisfaction, part of which may come from the danger of uprooting, part from increasing pressure from the nobility, which is itself threatened by the economic development. The nobility, of course, grows weaker as subsistence farming is replaced by cash-crop farming. The noble's story is one of hanging on politically while his economic underpinning gradually erodes. The clergy is also declining in power and influence as the process of secularization takes place. The middle class, merchants first, and later bankers and industrialists, grows more powerful as craftsmen, represented by guilds, strive to maintain a dominant position. The rise of the craftsmen, however, has come later in the feudal period and their economic foundations outlast those of the nobility. Unemployment is common, and a problem of what to do with the poor arises frequently. Occasionally the agrarian poor and its urban counterpart will rebel fiercely against employers or lords. Such rebellions are always suppressed with great brutality. Changing social relationships arouse jealousy and restlessness in all classes; increasing nominalism and economic changes are destroying the old reassuring and supporting traditions, while a prevailing, smug regionalism is challenged by an awareness of nationality and an increasing receptivity to new ideas. Philosophy challenges theological domination, causing the church to become more preoccupied with problems of heresy and schism. Internal reformations take place. Man is still concerned about God, but he is also concerned about his relation to other men and to his culture.

This is a period in which the application of feelings about religion to man creates a heroic style — strong on form and clarity, portraying types rather than the unique, lacking self-consciousness, and often possessing a beauty, simplicity and spirituality that is never surpassed in subsequent phases.

External contacts of the civilization are likely to increase along with external wars as the process of economic expansion sends explorers, traders and finally settlers beyond familiar areas. These adventurers are likely to bring back more in terms of cultural and economic material than they bestow upon alien civilizations and barbarians (defined in Chapter VI, "Conflict with Barbarians"), since they do not have much to give but have developed a strong desire to acquire. They can charm and cheat the barbarian, they can bully the rich but degenerate civilization, and they can derive aesthetic and intellectual benefits from the developed civilization even if they can neither fight it nor gain favorable terms of trade. The influence of these incursions is likely to be reflected in the development of new techniques, ideas and forms, borrowed from other civilizations but modified to fit the changing patterns of waning middle ages.

NOTES

a. Nation States and City States

The model seems more satisfactory for nation state systems than for city state systems. The city state separates itself from the feudal system long before the nation state. It develops its power on the basis of its ability to defend itself, not of its ability to extend its area of control. If a town stands alone, it will probably remain a feudal town, separate from the gentry but still restrained by feudal influences. But if it develops in relation to other towns, a different pattern will emerge. This will lead to an end of aristocracy in the town, a rapid secularization, the development of a tyranny or a republican form of government, a sophisticated system of diplomacy, manufacturing and trade, and a rapid, sometimes amazing culmination of aesthetics and ideas. But before a city state system can reconstitute itself it is likely to have such an impact on the transforming feudal system around it that it ends up being incorporated or divided by larger, ruder, more powerful states in its periphery. City states have not been effective, as a rule, in resisting larger peripheral states. One exception was the Phoenician cities, which managed to fend off the Assyrians for several centuries by maintaining strong navies, by avoiding alliances with enemies of the Assyrians, and by serving Mesopotamian civilization in general in its economic relations with Classical civilization.

b. Music Leaves no Footprints

We tend to make our aesthetic judgments on the basis of the artifacts remaining to us. This may leave us with a distorted impression of the superiority of Western music. All we have from other civilizations are the remnants of a few instruments. We do not know what they played, we can only guess at the rhythms, we cannot hear the voices, and we have no idea at all how much of a part of the total culture it was, or in what way it was integrated into the culture.

4: THE STATE SYSTEM

Any transitional period may be resolved by a reversion to the previous situation. In the case of a disintegrating feudal system, it may be that the political transformation is not made, that outer relationships are not established. Under such circumstances a new religious synthesis may take place, subsistence farming may return, and the feudal system — apparently the basic civilized system in times of crisis — may be restored.

On the other hand a pattern of effective secular central governments presiding over cash-crop economies may become dominant, and the feudal system may be replaced by a crystalized state system. The comparative historians have been weak in their treatment of state systems. Toynbee and Quincy Wright have drawn their generalizations from five systems: the modern European, the Italian Renaissance, the Hellenistic, the Greek City States, and the Ch'un Ch'iu-Contending States period in China. There have been many others, notably the Chinese between the Han and T'ang empires, India and South-East Asia throughout most of their history, Islamic history generally, and modern Latin America. Part of the problem is that it is difficult to decide whether a given system, like the Ch'un Ch'iu, has more feudal characteristics than centralized, or whether, as in the case of the Hellenistic states, you aren't dealing with a series of adjacent empires. I am going to include the state system in the model with the warning that it is the least adequately studied and probably the most subject to revision.

Once crystalization takes place, the international alignment becomes relatively stable. It is unusual for a major state to be added to the system, or to leave, or to be absorbed by others. The states reach a dynamic equilibrium in which war, trade and exchange of ideas are continuous but governed by established customs and procedures. Politically, a balance of power operates to keep any state from becoming predominant, since others will always combine against any one which threatens to acquire a disproportionate amount of strength. The system of international law and diplomacy becomes more highly elaborated and eventually codified.

Wars are fought by professional mercenaries for limited economic or political objectives. The armies are better organized than they were in the crystalized feudal period and may have less effect on the civilian population. Wars rising out of middle-class revolutions are likely to be more extensive and violent, but once the revolutions have won their objectives the pattern of warfare is likely to subside. The "breathers" between wars might best be described as truces breaking into the normal condition of war. Occasionally a grand settlement seems to be necessary to record the cumulative changes in power brought about by a series of wars. The wars fought between major powers are likely to be reproduced in colonial areas as the powers stake out rival claims.

The sovereign becomes a single hereditary leader, often a king. The monarch depends less on the aristocracy and calls more upon the rising bourgeoisie for advice and support. There is likely to be a professional administration, a centrally organized financial system, an elaborate national law requiring professional interpretation and considerably more internal stability than in the period of transition.

If, however, the middle class is denied access to political power or cramped in its development in other ways, it may seize this power by revolution. Ultimately the middle class acquires control of the country, and the king himself, if he manages to hold his throne, finds his power waning. If the king is replaced, he will be succeeded by a tyrant or a republic. Codifications of law, franchise bills, religious reforms, concordats and other symbols of adjustment and settlement are likely to appear at the conclusion of this middle-class assumption of power.

With greater stability and order in the home area, commerce becomes extremely important. Roads are built to encourage transportation within and between nations. Shipbuilding becomes a major industry. Explorers in search of exotic goods often perform amazing feats and the luxury goods they procure often bring merchants immense wealth. The state, in need of finances to support its more elaborate governmental apparatus, encourages trade by establishing a single currency and controling its production, and protecting trading posts and colonies set up in different territories. The colonies are regarded as outposts of the state and its inhabitants are expected to procure materials unavailable in the state, and to ship them "home."

Agriculture becomes more specialized as the trade of goods brings greater profits. It pays the farmer to concentrate on producing whatever his land is best adapted to, and buy the rest. Peasants become accustomed to making payments to the noble, the king or the state in money rather than in kind.

Accumulated capital from trading enterprises becomes available to support centralized industries, like ship-building and mining. The state takes an interest in production, subsidizing or controlling key industries and regulating imports from other states in such a way as to favor the establishment and maintenance of domestic industry.

Peasant dissatisfaction continues. Specialization continues to hamper them as land is appropriated for other purposes. At the same time the general stability of the state reduces the number of famines and the peasant population begins to increase. More and more of the children of peasants go to the towns to try to find employment. These add to the ranks of both the proletariat and the middle class.

The nobility is losing its political as well as economic influence. The sons of nobles tend to merge with the middle class. The upper clergy is also facing a loss of political and economic power. The town priests become more identified with the middle class and proletariat, more alienated from the church hierarchy.

The middle class seeks to wrest political advantage from the clergy and nobility. Members of the middle class are likely to receive more political and social distinction. If this is denied to them, they are likely to become dissatisfied and an intelligentsia emerges. This aggregate of merchants, officers, professional men, teachers, students, journalists and derailed nobility will build up increasing pressure for reformation until finally, by force or foresight, it takes place. Ultimately the middle class dominates the state. Town crafts continue to play a major part in production, but the craftsman is losing his social status. Entrepreneurs choose locations in towns where guild restrictions will not hamper them and the old ones often sink into provincial backwaters. The town is the backbone of the culture, but some are growing large, losing their original structure, influencing and receiving influences from regions far beyond their own, and thereby facing a new series of problems we generally associate with cities. The city in which the government is located becomes the capital and thereby the center of administration, transportation and culture. The network of communications now runs between cities and towns because it is in these that things are happening, that "history is being made."

The town family, though detached from the land, continues to be close-knit, maintaining a strong sense of family pride, possibly running a family business, and usually unified in at least the externals of religion. It is the rural family, torn by economic problems and the pull of towns and cities, that faces the threat of disintegration.

The crystalized state exists in a period of growing awareness, curiosity, self-consciousness. Men take more pride in themselves and think of themselves as relating to the world. They are consciously and unashamedly concerned about the material world and about improving their position in it. They are aware of the state to which they belong and they identify themselves more readily with its fortunes. They are convinced that the world they live in is a good one, a promising one, a better one than anyone else has, if they think very much about anyone else. Their tolerance of other ways is that of a secure and going world, not that of a world in search of revolutionary answers.

The process of secularization continues. Religious tolerance grows until the insistence upon the prevalence of one religious view over another comes to be regarded as fanaticism. The church continues for a while to play a useful role as counselor, consoler and administrator of rituals of birth, marriage and death.

This is likely to be a period of philosophical and scientific consolidation. Basic scientific and philosophical concepts are synthesized, the great thinkers of the civilization are likely to emerge. These men are not necessarily the most original or creative, but the men regarded as "great" are likely to be those who perceive the relationships in separate strands of creative thought. In some cultures emphasis may be on reason, on thinking problems through; in others on empiricism, on testing ideas in the laboratory or in the world. After the basic ideas have been set forth, there is likely to be a long period of elaboration and classification.

Aesthetic development reaches its culmination. Art and literature grow more conscious, less anonymous, technically more proficient and realistic, yet still imbued with much of the creative genius and sense of awe that characterized the archaic period. Great individual writers and masters of painting, architecture and composition arise at this time. The course of music follows a bit later. The emerging self-consciousness results in an increase in art and literary classification and criticism.

External contacts have resulted in the establishment of trading posts and finally settlements. These settlements may in time desire and even gain a degree of autonomy from the authority of their native state, particularly after they are governed by generations that have not been born in the mother country. They are likely to be primarily middle-class societies since it is difficult to carry feudal relationships in a boat. Relations between the settlers and the barbarians are likely to stabilize with the barbarians having to accept many of the vaues of the civilization and perhaps being assimilated by it. The crystalized civilization is relatively closed to external ideas; it projects more than it receives.

NOTES

a. The Neglect of State Systems

Why have comparative historians written more about feudal and imperial systems than about state systems? It may be that the latter are less easily defined than empires, or it may be that even for comparative historians it is less easy to see the system in which you are living as simply one among many. It may be difficult for publishers too, because Robert Wesson, whose study of empires was published in 1967, has had a difficult time finding a publisher for a companion volume on state systems. Publishers appear to regard it as if it were old hat. There have been a few comparative studies of empires, but Wesson's old hat will be the first comparative study of state systems — if it is ever accepted.

b. Revolutions as Watersheds

I have assumed until recently that the French Revolution was a significant watershed in Western history. And so it was. But in terms of the nature of the state system, middle-class revolutions provide adjustments that bring political and economic changes into line. Order may be lost for a time in the process, and warfare may become more violent, but that is the nature of adjustments. The changes that take place are logical within the framework of things as they exist. It is not so much a question of new forms being established as of encumbering forms being swept away. And if a relationship is maintained between political and economic power, revolution may be avoided.

c. Provincial Authority in a Crystalized State

While much is said in introductory histories about the consolidation of power in the emerging state, the more advanced and sophisticated histories are usually at pains to point out how much provincial authority is maintained. Towns and villages insist on running their own affairs in many ways and most central governments, having evolved reasonably satisfactory methods of collecting taxes, and policies that will generally permit economic growth, are content to allow the regions to solve their own problems. Usually the size of armies and the conditions of roads is such that the central government has no choice. This willingness of the regions to handle their own affairs is an indication of consolidation and crystalization of the system.

d. The Transportation of Class

A passage above concerning the difficulties of colonial settlers transporting class in a "boat" betrays a Classical-Western bias. Explorers and settlers may have no need for boats, but even so they will have difficulty taking their land relationships with them. When Ivan III gave the Zemschiks large plots of land from Moscow, he tore them from their seat of power. They may have remained nobles, but their sons could not command the respect their fathers had. Even today the electronics engineer who is the son of an old Newburyport family cannot easily take his class with him when he is transferred to Chicago.

5: THE TIME OF TROUBLES

The integration of a state system, like that of a feudal system. cannot last indefinitely. For a long time, depending partly on external conditions and partly on the luck and skill of the men who govern and negotiate, adjustments are made that keep the system operating efficiently enough to serve the majority of its inhabitants. But ultimately the state system too shows signs of needing a major overhaul, of losing its relevance to the major challenges of the times. Consciously or unconsciously men must decide whether the system is to be overhauled, replaced by some other kind of system, or allowed to ossify or disintegrate.

The crisis is most obviously reflected in the changing nature of relations between states. Diplomacy is circumvented more frequently and violations of international law occur more often. The sense of proportion concerning the relation of the military to the system is lost, arms expenditures increase disproportionately, and large standing armies are built up by all major powers.

The large armies sooner or later clash and the system of alliances is translated into a system of wars involving most of the civilization. These wars are sometimes halted by exhaustion peaces reminiscent of those following extensive religious wars of a transitional feudal period. But in the long run they may have a destructive effect on the lives, materials and spirit that compose the civilization itself. The situation may be resolved if a power, or a bloc of voters dominated by a single state, is successful in overthrowing the others and establishing an empire. Or it may be resolved if the weakened state system is conquered by a state from an alien system or dominated by newer, larger, more powerful peripheral nations that have been generated by the culture of the state system itself.

External wars are likely to increase as members of the system transfer hostilities during periods of arms building and tension, and also as barbarians, stimulated by ideas and techniques of their conquerors, struggle to apply them toward achieving their own self-government. Lacking wealth and technique, the barbarians resort to incessant guerrilla warfare, using all methods at their command to escape the civilization's physical dominance.

The desire for efficiency and order in an increasingly diverse society will lead to a general trend toward centralization in the management of taxation, in the control of local government, in the codification of law. Governments are likely to become more bureaucratic, to be managed by an efficient, loyal, harassed, permanent civil service. A large number of new institutions, government controlled or private, are likely to spring up in an effort to cope with increasingly complex and insoluble problems. These, however, ultimately have the effect of increasing the complexity and reducing the efficiency of the government itself. This situation encourages the rise of strong men — great simplifiers — to power. These men are likely to emerge on the basis of personalities that can be communicated to an increasingly worried, fretful lower middle class. Once they come to power, however, they may prove to be tyrants bent on destroying the outmoded apparatus in favor of simple and arbitrary procedures that fulfill their own personal ends rather than those of the state they profess to be serving.

The relative stability and efficiency of the state system eventually brings about a subtle internal economic crisis. The most immediate needs are satisfied, standards of living rise, a relatively large percentage of the townsmen become affluent. Production within the civilization turns more toward luxury goods and there is a leveling-off of investment in basic industries.

While these tendencies are manifesting themselves, areas outside the central civilization have been stimulated by its development. These peripheral and colonial areas begin to develop their own basic production, and once they have become established they become more efficient than the central areas.

These attempted adjustments are being made in an atmosphere in which things seem to be getting more and more out of joint. The incessant and increasingly violent warfare of the Time of Troubles begins to interfere with commerce, to destroy to some extent existing productive capacity, and to force nations to devote a higher percentage of their production to implements of war. This leads to a leveling-off of living standards and a tendency for major producers to depend on government military needs as a permanent source of demand. The central economic system becomes more subjected to fluctuations of price, to hyper-inflations and deflations, and to unemployment. Governments are more concerned and less effective in attempting to control prices and bring relief.

Through the entire period of the state system agriculture has become the task of a smaller percentage of the population as industrialization improves farming methods. Farms are controlled more from the cities by an urban educated middle class, and they tend to become ever larger and more specialized.

The increase complexity of relationships between commerce, industry and agriculture, the large percentage of people engaged in non-food producing activities, the increasing vulnerability of the system to internal fluctuations and external competition, and the increasing damaging effects of war lead to recurrent breakdowns with a resultant tendency in some areas toward a return to self-sufficiency by garden farming for home consumption and by the return of subsistence industries.

Classes undergo such an amalgamation that it is difficult to sort them out under the old terminologies. The nobility and clergy lose their importance, sometimes disappear as a class. However when tyrants come to power they sometimes maintain "courts" on a basis somewhat similar to that of the early monarchs who raised members of the bourgeoisie to noble positions.

Peasants are declining in numbers, either falling to the proletariat class or rising to join the middle-class farmers, themselves employers of others. The civil service forms a larger part of the middle-class elite as the government comes to control more of the society's functions. The military also forms an important part of this governmental elite. The working class remains always material for politics but never itself becomes an innovating political factor. Working-class economic standards continue to improve until the economic system begins to suffer breakdown. Then unemployment and consequent suffering may increase considerably. If the condition continues, the working class may either become predatory, or perish, or return to the countryside to seek employment under neo-feudal conditions. Demagogues arising from the lower middle class find powerful support in this proletariat.

The intelligentsia, which had its origins among the middle class, is likely to disappear once middle-class opportunities are achieved, but it is likely to reappear among the lower middle classes and in the upper ranks of the proletariat if the economic apparatus begins to function badly. It is also likely to appear in the peripheral areas of the civilization or in the barbarian areas where a rising middle class is denied political or economic opportunity by alien overlords.

Great cities develop, reducing the towns to provincial insignificance as they attract like moths the strongest and most enterprising from the countryside. These cities lose contact with the areas around them and ultimately destroy their own sources of material and spiritual rejuvenation. The cosmopolitan urbanites, separated from the rural environment, develop a restless, anti-domestic ethos. Families are smaller, since children are no longer necessary to perpetuate family businesses. The family disintegrates, children find their own way and often live far from parents and relatives, divorce becomes more common since there is no particular reason for holding a family together. Ultimately population growth begins to level off and in central areas even to decline.

Materialism continues to increase as a bourgeois taste for luxury and comfort occupies a larger place in everyday life to the exclusion of upper class traditions of service and honor. But there are also signs of dissatisfaction with the products of wealth as tastes become jaded and materialism as such is depreciated by the intelligentsia.

Leaders become more and more ruthless. But as the state loses its popularity, leaders direct their ruthlessness more to personal ends and they cease, as the people do, to care about the state as such. Ruthlessness also increases at all levels of competition as individuals become more pragmatic in seeking means to achieve private ends, less concerned about the cost of the means.

Humanism wanes as the human being is seen in mechanistic, impersonal terms. The attitude Spengler calls cosmopolitanism is by nature concerned with ideas and transient fashions rather than emotions and the enduring characteristics of man. Non-involvement with personalities is considered a virtue. Human types easily become interchangeable in a rootless environment in which people are constantly on the move and constantly meeting new faces. It becomes more difficult for the individual to identify with place or people, more difficult to find inner form and meaning in an ever-changing world of evanescent fashion.

This leads to a general weariness with social, public and world affairs and a longing for repose, calm, peace.

The cosmopolitan attitude finds its counterpart in a scientific and philosophical preoccupation with criticism, classification and detailed, refined, specialized investigation. Since this leads to the narrow and particular, while problems are becoming broad and general, alternative approaches are more frequently employed: either emphasis is placed on the irrational, romantic and intuitive, or else scientists, philosophers, theologians and men of affairs pursue synthesis, finding universal factors in rival philosophies and in human relations. Artists and writers become preoccupied with trying to find new forms, since the styles of the crystalized period are becoming exhausted. Much that was significant has become elaborated, enlarged to the point of colossalism or watered down into comparative formlessness for mass consumption. Thus although the period is rich in ideas, whether the artists succeed in finding appropriate forms to express them probably depends on whether the civilization itself achieves reconstitution.

This is a period of active and confused relationships with peripheral and alien territories. Peripheral territories may dominate the mother civilization. Colonists and barbarians seek independence. The peripheral, colonial and barbarian areas are likely to have competitive relationships with one another. But within the core of civilization there is an open tolerance of barbarian and alien values and forms.

In this painful and exciting period the city is central through government and economic, cultural and intellectual activity, and as the home of the dominating middle class. Its inhabitants live lives utterly divorced from the close relation to the countryside of earlier times. In its great monuments and limitless spread, the great city expresses the colossalism and formlessness of its period.

NOTES

a. Wars and Peaces

If the conflicts of 1914-18 and 1939-45 were wars, the quieter periods that preceded, separated and followed should be regarded as peaces. If it sounds odd or amusing to ask whether the peaces of Germany have been longer or more fragmented than the peaces of France, it must be, as Downing Bowler observes, that we usually think of peace as the general condition, a medium of history on which wars are occasionally etched.

b. *Flash-in-the-Pan Empires*

Sometimes empires which seem to have resolved the problems generated by war are quickly overthrown. If this happens it is because there is sufficient feeling that the state system, for all its shortcomings, still is worth saving and reviving: attitudes of national loyalty are stronger than the weariness of war. The ephemeral empires of Alexander and Napoleon are obvious examples; the Maurya empire, the Srivijayan empire of Indonesia and the Islamic caliphates would probably be less obvious cases of this kind.

c. *Urban "Draining of the Countryside"*

This has been a recurrent phenomenon, but the Western reinvasion of the countryside seems to be a result of the Faustian pattern and the extraordinary population increase. We have seen people leaving the city before. The Romans had their country villas to which they could retire for relief from urban tensions. But Westerners bring the city with them to the country when they escape it. I moved out of town recently myself. It is rather pleasing to be located where you can easily step in horse manure and where your dog can encounter a skunk. But we watched the urban world series for a while yesterday on our urban television set and called the urban plumber on our urban telephone this morning because our urban indoor toilet is not functioning properly.

I think we shall have to go away for a month this summer to "get away from it all."

d. *Population Growth*

Writing about the leveling-off of population seems out of place in a world in which population has risen from two to three billion in less than four decades. But this has been the trend in urbanizing areas of other civilizations, and it was the trend in the West from 1870 to 1940. The present reversal of trend could be an indication of reconstitution or it could be a temporary fluctuation that will be halted by the concern it is causing. Most of the population increase, of course, is taking place in the non-Western world, which is in a different phase of development.

e. *Museums and Zoos*

Christopher Dawson has pointed out the resemblance. Both are collections of the alien, both succeed remarkably in distorting because of contexts and juxtapositions, and the exhibits in both are seen and wondered at, but rarely correlated with one's own experiences.

6: The Imperial System

The problems of the transitional state system may be resolved by reconstitution or by transition to empire. In periods of extreme conflict it would seem possible that a state system would revert to feudalism, but the comparative historians say little about this and I have not found any clear examples. Perhaps the reversion does not take place because the forms of government that have been learned make centralization a more natural solution to problems. Perhaps reversion has occurred, but among the smaller, less well known political entities within state systems. When reconstitution or transition take place, there will be a trend toward stability and integration of patterns. In the case of reconstitution, another period of relatively crystalized state system will follow. If the transition leads to the formation of an empire, there are likely to be some parallels to the state system, but in many ways an imperial system represents a distinctly different kind of development.

The imperial system is brought about by total conquest. This will be followed by a period of civil power wars until an image of government stability is built up, which must take at least a generation or more probably two. Once authority is firmly established over the empire, a golden age of internal peace follows.

War and diplomacy still take place, but they are remote from the lives of most inhabitants. Diplomacy is carried on with external powers while marginal barbarian wars and limited wars with other empires, or powers from other civilizations, are carried on by the small, mobile, professional armies.

The government is despotic, headed by an emperor who resembles the hereditary monarch. Institutions are simplified, a streamlined civil service being the most important administrative body. The most effective empires are likely to permit an increasing amount of provincial authority. Too much centralized authority stifles development and creates resentment and discontent.

The development of internal peace and the creation of a large free trading area greatly encourage commerce and industry. The government is likely to support this development by the construction of roads, irrigation projects and other "social overhead" projects. The high level of specialization possible in an empire enables it to produce a wide variety of finished products efficiently and it is therefore likely to increase trade with barbarians and alien societies. But it does not depend on this trade for its welfare. Industry is likely to develop most efficiently at a regional level. Large manufacturers either break up or delegate total authority to provincial managers. Standards of living are high and distribution of wealth relatively widespread.

The empire is essentially a middle class society. Civil servants, industrialists, specialists of various kinds form the bulk of the ruling elite. The academic and military professions play a much smaller part. There is a lower middle class and a skilled proletariat. These are not easily distinguishable or particularly class-conscious. The unskilled proletariat is likely to find employment on a fairly regular basis and lead a fairly secure life. The intelligentsia is minimal and ineffectual. All in all, this is a a society of "respectable" people.

While all roads lead to Rome, and Rome is likely to be a glamorous metropolis and center of power, there will probably be many other cities that have a special regional importance in an urbanized countryside. The latter term does not mean that trees and sky have disappeared but that the people living in the country have essentially urban ways of looking at things and prefer urban life. The desire men have to get away from urban tensions is better solved by reservations of countryside in the cities (parks, wild commons, wildlife reservations) and by the custom of taking remote vacations (including vacations away from a villa or cottage originally established for the purpose of taking vacations).

The civilization simmers down. People are generally materialistic but there is a great concern about "taste." It is not good form to be too demonstrative or exhibitionistic. There is an emphasis on manners, sensibleness, moderation. There is also a good deal of conformity, although nonconformity is considered reasonable in prescribed areas. Ritualism is strong in religion and other areas of life, but feelings are held in check. Stoicism is admired, lamentation causes embarrassment. There is a closed tolerance toward the activities of others as long as they do not threaten the culture. Privacy is respected. The universality of man is held up as an ideal but it is not good form to fight about it. The culture could be described as bland, subtle or tired, depending on the standpoint from which it is seen.

Philosophy reaches a relatively tranquil period. A synthesis of ideas has been reached and there are relatively few new hypotheses. Emphasis is placed on ethics, standards of conduct, the good life. Religion and government are reunited, but the church's role is one of support in times of individual trouble and service in times of individual fortune. Religious minorities are ignored or regarded with amusement. Education becomes more vocational, more directed toward the culture in which it exists, less widespread. Standards at higher levels can be rigorous and the best scholars exhibit a remarkable capacity for the assimilation and organization of knowledge.

Certain forms of art seem to become acceptable, to meet the standards of good taste. These may be traditional or they may be modern so long as they are not "way out." Codes of ethics, morals and taste are often imposed by the government, and these impositions are accepted as proper. This is not a creative period: the writer or painter who attempts to move outside accepted standards will find himself without a market.

Relations outside the civilization are tranquil in this period. Wars are primarily concerned with secondary adjustments. Trade is useful and profitable but not extensive or essential. Ideas outside the civilization tend to be similar as peripheral areas seeks emulation. Alien civilizations may derive ideas from the empire, but its inhabitant are not likely to be receptive to an overflow of ideas from beyond the pale.

The transformations of form and idea described here will vary, of course, according to the patterns of a particular civilization. One possible variation is that the political transformation to empire will be delayed, or never completed. It may be that the expansionary forces of a transitional state system are so explosive that a resulting empire proves to be overexpanded, and breaks down into several manageable political entities. This will look like an enlarged state system, but the structure of each entity will be more like that of an empire than a state, and conflict between them more or less on a personal rather than national level. Such a system is likely to be rather fragile. The Hellenistic system may have been an example.

The political decentralization of an empire may also serve as a method of attaining reconstitution as it did in Diocletian's time. As Toynbee has pointed out, empires have strong propensities to reconstitute themselves, even under alien rulers. They very rarely, possibly never, revert to state systems once they have become established. If they can no longer be made to go as imperial systems, a conversion to feudalism is likely to occur.

NOTES

a. The Placid Empire

The model here does not fit the circus-and-barbarian model sometimes associated with the Roman empire. But circuses were not as central or violent in the integrated period of that empire either, nor were "barbarians" barbaric.

b. Some More Zoo Theory

Imperial zoos differ from transitional zoos. They are more concerned with realism than with amazement. They try to put the animals in as natural an environment as possible. There are fewer animals and they are likely to be of a less spectacular kind. People go to transitional zoos hoping for education and relaxation, not stimulation.

7: Does the Model Work?

In the whimsical opening of *The Evolution of Civilizations,* Carroll Quigley recalls his boyhood hunt for quartz crystals that resembled the hexagonal prisms described in books. He rarely found them because they were almost always transformed by compression. "The fact that 99 per cent are distorted," he concluded, "does not deter the scientist from forming in his mind an idealized picture of an undistorted crystal, or from stating, in books, that quartz crystals occur in that idealized form."

When we turn to civilizations, we cannot find even the one per cent, because there are no more than a dozen examples on which there is reasonable agreement (see Chapter I, section 6). These are the Chinese, Japanese, Indian, Mesopotamian, Islamic, Egyptian, Cretan, Classical, Byzantine, Western, Middle American and Andean.

Now it is certain that the model does not describe any of these twelve civilizations. But if the model is valid, it ought to describe the majority of civilizations in any of its particular aspects. Where it fails to do this, the model should be modified. To test it in each of its aspects against history would require several more volumes. So I am going to limit myself to a test of the single, most obvious, most verifiable aspect of the model: political form.

In how many of these civilizations is there actually a transition from feudal through imperial political forms? The process is clear enough as a single sequence only in a single civilization: the Andean. Here there is little question that a typical river-valley feudal system was transformed into a multiple state system of which the Chimu and Inca states were the largest. Finally the Incas succeeded in conquering all the other states and forming an empire.

In Chinese, Japanese, Indian and Egyptian history the process repeats itself. The feudal Shang-Chou period gradually transforms itself into the state system of the Ch'un Ch'iu and Contending States periods and then into the Han Empire. A feudal period is well established long before the final fall of the later Han. This feudal period once again takes on the aspects of a state system in the fourth century, and in the seventh a second imperial phase is launched under the T ang. After that Chinese history is anomalous, with the imperial phase dominant.

The Japanese go through a similar consolidation culminating in the unified state of the Heian-Kyoto period. This breaks down into feudalism under the Kamakura Shogunate and after that feudal and state patterns are difficult to untangle. But the Tokugawa Shogunate emerges clearly enough as a second imperial phase.

Indian history is more divided, the feudal period of the Indus River merging into a long period of state rivalry, the Maurya dynasty representing an unsuccessful attempt at unification that is finally realized under the Gupta emperors. Breakdown to feudalism follows, large states like the Delhi Sultanate and Bahmini Kingdom arise, and unification recurs under the Mughal Empire.

Egypt experiences a divided period before the establishment of the Old Kingdom. The reversion to feudalism that follows continues through the Middle Kingdom. But unification recurs under the New Kingdom.

Both the Inca and Mughal empires are themselves conquered by aliens: the Spaniards and the British. This pattern of Alien Empire also holds for three other civilizations: the Mesopotamian, Byzantine and Middle American. These three civilizations clearly experience feudal and state phases. In the case of Mesopotamia the city states of the earlier period are later replaced by larger states. The Byzantine feudal period is like that of the later Han, arising out of a disintegrating empire. But the imperial phases of each of these three civilizations are provided by alien conquerors: the Persians, Ottomans and Spaniards.

Islam seems to have lacked the political temperament for an imperial state. Various caliphates attain considerable size, but soon break up. Even the Ottomans are not able to control the Islamic world for more than a few decades.

Data on the Cretan civilization, as far as I know, is not adequate. There is a feudal period, all right, and there are separate cities, but their relationship to Knossos is not clear.

Classical civilization had a pattern of transition from Greek city states to the greater Hellenistic states to empire. But a pattern of independent farming lacking the usual feudal political relationships seems to have existed in the earliest periods of Classical history.

Western civilization has clearly discernable feudal and state systems, but no imperial period. The data on this civilization, however, is not yet all in.

It would appear that eight of the twelve have gone through at least one cycle of feudal, state and imperial forms. Four of them experience a second cycle, although when that happens the feudal and state phases tend to get muddled. Classical civilization appears to have lacked a feudal system, Crete and possibly Egypt may not have had state systems, and Islam, Crete (probably) and the West (so far) lack imperial systems. The correlation between the model and the political forms actually experienced in the individual civilizations seems to be fairly high.

In constructing this model, I have deliberately ignored the formidable complications that arise when civilizations come into contact with one another. The model assumes a general freedom to develop without external influence. But in fact civilizations are constantly coming in contact with one another, often impeding or deflecting and sometimes destroying one another. Moreover one civilization, the Western, seems to be in the process of overwhelming the entire face of the earth and superceding all civilizations that have ever existed.

How much does this interaction of civilizations modify the hypothesis? And even if a modified hypothesis emerges, does it have any relevance in a world that seems to be overrun by Faustian Man? These questions must be considered before any hypothesis on the nature of civilizations can be considered adequate for sacrificial offering.

VI

WHEN CIVILIZATIONS COLLIDE

1: Transmission Between Civilizations

The internal consistency of the patterns of any civilization is likely to be muddled by fortuitous encounters with other civilizations. It is difficult to determine how much a civilization originates and how much it borrows, or whether it is likely to be more susceptible to external influences at some stages than at others. But however much of a nuisance these encounters may appear to be to the scholar who would like to put his civilizations on a laboratory table, they greatly increase possibilities for elaboration and reconstitution. Without these encounters there would be fewer civilizations and most of them would be less richly developed if not ossified, because new thematic material so often comes from the process of assimilating alien ideas and artifacts.

The extent to which civilizations incorporate external material depends first on the relevance of the material, second on the receptivity of the civilization and last on the force with which the material is presented.

If an alien technique is relevant, it may be accepted pretty nearly intact. But the alien civilization has not thereby changed the receiving civilization very much; it has merely supplied a convenient institution. If the institution had not been available, something serving the same purpose might have been reinvented. Many implements, as Kroeber shows, have been reinvented several times or have been invented in different parts of the same civilization as the need arises (*Anthropology,* Ch. 11, pp. 445-473).

The transmission of ideas is not likely to be so easy, since an idea must be understood in the context of its development. But alien ideas may provide keys to problems that the ideas of one's own culture, perhaps limited and influenced by one another, have failed to solve. The alien ideas then may open the door to new inferences, but these will be worked out within the context of domestic traditions and approaches, so that in the end they will probably bear little resemblance to their source. A religion developed in one civilization — Christianity and Buddhism are obvious examples — may find greater acceptance in another civilization partly because it *is* alien, because it offers something fresh that cannot be developed in a civilization enmeshed in its own traditions.

A thing can be altered in terms of materials available, but it must still be able to perform the function for which it was borrowed. A plow may be pulled by a man or a horse, it may be made of wood or iron, but it must plow. An idea may be turned upside down. "All men are equal" may mean all men are free or all men are slaves. But even in the case of techniques, the function is much easier to transmit than the manner of functioning. Transmission of plowing is one thing; transmission of the style of plowing is something else.

A civilization is much more likely to be receptive to external material in its transitional phases, when institutions and ideas in general are open to reassessment. But even in crystalized periods there are always some institutions in need of revision, and solutions for this revision may come from alien sources.

When a civilization is in a receptive phase, ideas may be more readily absorbed than techniques. Techniques, while more readily adaptable if they are relevant, are pointless if they are not. But ideas can be amazingly transformed: Christianity was able to meet the needs first of Classical civilization in disintegration, then of Western civilization in transformation.

The most important transitional period is the formative one, that which leads to the development of a feudal culture that is distinctly "new." Alien intrusions in these formative periods can shape patterns that will last as long as the civilization itself. Subsequent transitional periods may absorb alien influences that will contribute to the reconstitution of a civilization, but not to its reshaping. A transition from a feudal system to a state system or a reconstitution of a state system must involve the retaining of many patterns. If all central patterns are demolished — the religious, social and economic — the civilization is likely to revert to feudalism, to make a fresh start as something new.

The importance of the force with which techniques and ideas are disseminated has been stressed only by Toynbee. It seems probable that, setting aside physical force for a moment, the phase of the receiving civilization is more important than that of a transmitting one. When a civilization has a strong internal image, when its institutions are working well in relation to one another, external techniques and ideas will be cheerfully tolerated as irrelevant and inferior. The Manchu dynasty was not interested in Western nations; Colbert could not persuade his fellow Frenchmen of the importance of being concerned with the world outside of Europe.

The rise to power of the Soviet Union has stimulated the study of Russian history, and this provides a particularly relevant example of the interaction of civilizations. Students of Russian history are agreed that whether or not Russia is a civilization itself, it is at any rate derived from a non-Western civilization. And there is a fairly strong agreement among students of Russian history (less among students of Soviet government) that Western socialism has been translated into a Russian form that is congenial to traditions of autocracy and orthodoxy. Russian civilization was undergoing changes that made it receptive to Western techniques and ideas, which were, however, transformed out of all recognition when put into practice. The study of Marx is probably less relevant to an understanding of the Soviet Union than the study of the adoption of the Byzantine religion and the subsequent Mongol invasion — earlier alien intrusions that helped shape formative patterns, whereas socialism provided only a means toward reconstitution. Thus we see Russian civilization adopting what is relevant and reshaping it to fit patterns that are long established, patterns too basic to be desroyed without destroying the civilizaion itself.

Notes

a. Cultures and the Cow

Though ideas are more transmutable than things, the patterns of a civilization can be so powerful that the most ordinary things can function in the most remarkably different ways. What could be more mundane, ubiquitous and immutable than a cow? Yet Europeans use cows to supply both dairy products and meat. Hindus, regarding cows as sacred, milk them but do not slaughter them. The Chinese slaughter them for meat, but don't use them for any dairy products. Eating dairy products is not in the Chinese culture pattern. They just don't like milk.

b. Spengler's Mutually Exclusive Civilizations

Poor old Spengler has been castigated for insisting that each civilization is absolutely separate from all others. Actually he grants that forms can be translated but insists that they will be received only superficially. "Connotations are not transferable" (*The Decline of the West*, II: 57). In a sense it is very difficult for one individual to get his own ideas across to others even in the same civilization, as every teacher knows when he reads his blue books and as every writer knows when he reads his reviews. How impossible, then, for the complexities of a civilization to be translated to another. Spengler was right.

c. Does Necessity Produce Inventions?

Yes, of course. Irrigation, wherever it appears, takes on almost identical forms. If the rate of flow is too fast, erosion will occur. If too slow, the water will not reach the crops. Hence, if problems of desiccation are to be solved by irrigation, the solution will always be almost identical (Victor von Hagen, *The Realm of the Incas*, p. 72). But is invention inevitable? No. The solution to a problem may never be found. Then if it's a minor problem the civilization will live with it, as it has with famine, plague and war. If it is central, the civilizaton will be destroyed or dispersed.

d. Toynbee's Concept of Cultural Radiation

Some writers, Toynbee in particular, contend that civilizations in disintegration transmit political and economic forms earlier and more effectively than aesthetics and ideas. Sorokin replies that if anything it is the other way around, that political and economic techniques lag behind the ideas preparing the way for their acceptance. I think that Toynbee is right to the extent that civilizations in transition are more likely to be expansive, and that the explorers and traders leading the expansion would be better qualified to demonstrate physical techniques. But so much more depends on the phase and patterns of the receiving civilization that it is useless to cite examples (Sorokin, *Philosophies*, pp. 299-305; Toynbee, *Study*, V: 198-201).

2: CONFLICT BETWEEN CIVILIZATIONS

But what if one civilization is conquered by another? In this case it might not matter what phase the receiving civilization is in, it might be compelled to sacrifice its own patterns and accept those that are externally imposed. Just as unexpected death may cut a man off from his course of development, so a culture may be cut off by the unexpected emergence of another that is physically more powerful. The impact of Western civilization on those of Mexico and Peru provides striking examples.

But a culture is much harder to kill than a man. A vital culture can recover from military defeat, even apparent annihilation. The Ottoman state, completely overcome by the army of Timur Lenk, within fifty years had entirely recovered and resumed the conquest of Byzantium with which it had been occupied. The unexpected annihilation of its armies and carrying off of its Sultan in an iron cage appeared, in retrospect, to have been merely a bothersome interruption. Military conquest is not sufficient to subdue a vital culture. Why should it be? The advantages always lie with the conquered. They are in their home territory, living under their own customs. The conquerors must continue to govern their own lands and have usually only limited numbers of governors to spare. These must either retain ties with their own land, in which case they cannot influence the conquered peoples, or dedicate themselves to the conquered land, in which case they are likely to absorb more of the culture of the conquered than they impart.

But suppose the conquerors pursue a vigorous policy of cultural suppression? The Incas used to remove rebellious populations from the land and rewrite their history. In the contemporary Western world we have seen attempts to isolate sub-cultures and even to obliterate them. Cannot a vital culture be wiped out if its pattern is completely broken and remains broken for a long period? If the conqueror controls all the conquered, reeducates them for a period of seventy years so that no living person remembers the old culture, and destroys in this period all recorded history, cannot a pattern of civilization then be destroyed, no matter how vital it might have been?

Probably. There is nothing mystical about culture patterns and probably they can be destroyed regardless of their vitality. Civilized sub-cultures and even nations have been virtually destroyed, but civilizations as a whole are such complex entities that they have proved virtually indestructible once their patterns are well established. So far there has been no case of a civilization in such a phase being destroyed by another. When a civilization has been destroyed, its patterns have already been in disintegration, as was the case with the American civilizations, or else it was in the process of formation, as is the case with those civilizations Toynbee designates as "abortive."

The suppression of an emerging civilization by one that is already developed has been called "pseudomorphosis" by Spengler. Because a large and powerful civilization is already in existence and occupying part of the territory that would otherwise be available for expansion, the incipient civilization is distorted and forced to follow anomalous patterns. The suppressed civilization is squeezed both in form and in development of ideas. It may even be occupied by its powerful neighbor, but it will persist in finding forms applicable to its own stage of development or transforming the characteristics of the overlying culture. Spengler identified such a civilization in the Middle East and called it the "Magian" culture. No one else has agreed with him, but it may be that the Middle East has been constantly distorted by the Sumeric, Classical, Islamic and Western civilizations to the extent that it is not easy to determine the origins and development of the cultures that have occupied the area. While it is hard to identify a recognizable civilization in this area, it does seem that it has long been an area in which civilized people have lived.

Now that Faustian transportation and communications have uncovered all possible areas of development, the phenomenon of pseudomorphosis may become more common. If new civilizations are to emerge, they may have to develop entirely in an area dominated by another civilization. Suppose, for instance, that a world state came into being which had the qualities of lassitude commonly associated with empire. Perhaps it would be possible for a new culture, bearing all the characteristics of the early phases of civilization — ritualistic religion, epic, feudalism, etc. — to develop within the confines of the old. This might be interpreted as rebellion by the central government or as evidence of reconstitution by the historian. But after a period of time it might become evident that a new civilization, having no relation to the old empire, has emerged. If it were not suppressed by the waning civilization, it would sooner or later reach a point of development in which it would become the new center of aesthetics and learning and eventually, perhaps with considerable conflict resulting, an independent political center as well.

Previously, as Toynbee points out (*Study Of History,* III: 365-377), civilizations have tended to develop in isolation from others. It is only logical that the best chance for development occurs in areas that are remote enough to be left alone, once an initial impetus has been established. When civilizations do develop in isolation, they are easier to identify and follow. It may be that the civilizations of the future, however, being much more under the influence of existing civilizations, will be as muddled as the Middle East and therefore more difficult to classify. The Middle Eastern pattern may simply represent a prototype of civilizations to come, and may no longer seem so incomprehensible when we have other examples to compare it with.

Obviously the phenomena of encounters between civilizations create problems for comparative historians but they do not seriously interfere with the study and comparison of individual civilizations. The more complex a culture is, the more it tends to maintain its own form despite external influences. It takes a very great external force to upset or terminate the development of a civilization. Despite transmission, despite conquest, despite pseudomorphosis, civilizations tend to maintain their identity. What they assimilate depends much more on what they are than on what is presented to them. Generally conquest does not destroy a vital civilization. And while a strongly established civilization can weigh heavily on a newly developing one, the two can nevertheless be distinguished.

NOTES

a. Was the Peruvian Civilization Obliterated?

The "destruction" of the American civilizations by the Spaniards is the most frequently cited example of the sudden termination of development because of fortuitous external forces.

But the destruction of the Incas is one thing; the obliteration of the civilization they governed is another. Julian Steward suggests that the Peruvian culture did not change materially in the transition from Incan to Spanish rule. Native chieftains were retained by the Spaniards and village activities were not disturbed. The bureaucracies of both conquerors required tribute of goods and services, though the Spaniards were more interested in gold. But goods for home consumption were not greatly changed. And while communities accepted first the Inca Sun God and then the Spanish Christian God, their local gods, cults and rites were not disturbed by the religious leaders of either empire (*Theory of Culture Change*, p. 59). From this viewpoint the Peruvian case, far from being an anomaly, looks like one of many examples of the ease with which imperial systems change their rulers.

b. Do Civilizations "Rise Again"?

Toynbee thinks so. He believes if they have been "prematurely cut short by alien conquerors" they are capable of "going to earth, hibernating for centuries" and eventually emerging to pick up where they left off (*Study of History*, VII: 78). Thus a Middle Eastern civilization reasserts itself, after a millennium, as an Islamic heir to a Persian Empire that had not been granted the centuries to which it was entitled. An Arabic society, in the nineteenth century, disentangles itself from its "sister" Iranic society after three hundred years of Ottoman domination. Mexican and Peruvian cultures, totally obliterated by the West, may any day now pounce upon the Juntas and Caudillos of South America (*Study*, VIII: 465; IV: 113-114).

Well, Toynbee is a charming man and a delightful writer. Who else would have had the check? Can't you just imagine Somervell trying to defend these doctrines at cocktail parties?

But it does seem that any civilized culture that carries a strong sense of history and internal vitality can transmit itself for many generations despite the loss of physical territory. The history of the Poles over the past two hundred years is a sufficient demonstration of this. And the preservation of Jewish culture is hardly less remarkable than anything Toynbee has envisioned.

c. Preservation Versus Development

It is important to ask whether a civilization recovering from externally imposed disaster is really continuing its development or whether the experience has forced it to encase itself within a cake of custom. Toynbee neatly draws the distinction (*Study*, abridged ed., I: 111) :

When the French recovered the battered shell of Reims cathedral they performed a pious restoration of each shattered stone and splintered statue. When the Athenians found the Hekatompedon burnt down to its foundations, they left the foundations lie and proceeded, on a new site, to build the Parthenon.

The Polish Baroque restoration of Warsaw looked like cultural encistment; cf. also Coventry cathedral in England, which is a highly self-conscious artistic/symbolic bit of both. The subsequent activity of Polish writers, however, would seem to indicate that perhaps the old structure must be resurrected as a symbol, but that development can go on from there.

3: THE REASONS FOR CONFLICT

Why do civilizations come into conflict? There is a rich assortment of theories to choose from in trying to answer this one. Is it because of an innate hostility that exists between people of basically different cultures, as Spengler believes? Or is it, as Sorokin contends, that such hostility emerges only when the central values of neighboring civilizations are basically incompatible? Or does it have something to do with differences in phase of development, as Nikolai Danilevsky and Flinders Petrie believed, and as Shepard Clough and Carroll Quigley believe today? Or is it simply a matter of differences in techniques, as emphasized by Quincy Wright? Or shall we look, as Toynbee does, at the internal causes for the expansion of civilizations?

When the Europeans went to India and China they traded more than they fought, or if they fought, it was to protect and develop their trade. But when the Europeans went to Mexico and Peru, they fought and conquered. If they were hostile to the Aztecs, why were they not hostile to the Chinese? I don't think the Europeans stopped to ask about the values of the alien civilizations. But they did see that they could conquer the American civilizations and that they could not conquer the Asian. The technological factors are clearly important. Where civilizations come upon one another suddenly, and where one proves to be technologically superior, the temptations of an easy conquest will be strong. Where there are no possibilities of conquest, a trading relationship is likely to develop, since each civilization is likely to have products otherwise unobtainable to the other. This was the case in the early European contacts with the Far East. Where civilizations come in contact and establish a power relationship, their attitudes toward one another will not differ greatly from attitudes among the sovereign states of a civilization toward each other.

Innate hostility between civilizations, if it exists, would seem to arise out of the fear of the unknown. Differences in values may establish a consciousness of separateness and thereby frame a possible object of attack. Differences between civilizations are likely to be greater than differences between states of the same civilization, particularly if the civilizations have developed in isolation and come upon one another suddenly. Western civilization responded to a deeply felt Islamic threat in both the Saracen and the Ottoman phases. Frequently European enemies allied to meet the threat.

Often, however, internal threats seem more imperative than those offered from other civilizations. Francis I didn't hesitate to ally himself with the Turks in his political struggles with Charles V, and this when the Ottomans were mounting their supreme threat to Europe, threatening the gates of Vienna itself. But Sulieman the Magnificent was the enemy of Charles and so was Francis and an alliance with your neighbor's neighbor is perfectly normal in international politics. And the kind of threat posed by the Ottomans to sixteenth-century Europe, or the Russians to twentieth-century Europe, is no greater, perhaps not so great, as the threats posed by the France of Napoleon or the Germany of Hitler. A Sulieman or a Stalin might acquire Budapest as an outpost, but the European leaders controlled a Paris or a Berlin as the very center of their operations.

Suppose civilizations come upon one another in different phases of development? A young civilization in an expanding, developing phase may very well overcome an older, disintegrating civilization, particularly if the older civilization has acquired a great deal of wealth, and assuming that the younger civilization has developed an adequate technology. But the development of techniques depends partly on the particular inclinations of a civilization, partly on its contacts with its neighbors. If the contact is gradual, the growing civilization will raise its techniques to the level of the older civilization, and perhaps will have more inclination to use them. But if the meeting is sudden, and if the older civilization should prove to have vastly superior techniques, it may be revived by the threat and moved to conquer. Whether such a conquest could be maintained would depend on whether the attack precipitated a major reconstitution in the older cvilization, and on the vitality and patterns of development of the younger civilization.

All conflict does not come about because of relationships between civilizations. Some of it may be attributable to a particular civilization's internal patterns or phase of development. It may be that the civilization has an inbuilt pattern of militarism. But such a civilization is likely to dissipate its energies in chronic warfare and is not likely to last too long in intercivilizational conflict. The Babylonian civilization in its Assyrian phase appears to have been one of these.

Civilizations in the developing stages of their state systems are likely to be characterized by a good deal of internal warfare. This warfare does not seem to diminish the vitality of the participating states and they may even have enough energy to turn their attention to states in civilizations not involved in their system. The states in this system are expanding, confident, certain of their abilities and their superiority. Wherever they find power vacuums they are likely to expand.

And I think there is no doubt that Toynbee is right in linking geographical expansion with disintegration. States involved in a time of troubles are likely to seek external conquests as a substitute for the adjustment of internal problems. Great conquerors who do not recognise the bounds of crystalized systems are likely to emerge in such periods. Once a reconstitution or transition to empire is effected, such expansionary tendencies are likely to die down.

NOTE

Expansion as an Indicator of Disintegration

Toynbee has been challenged by Sorokin and Christopher Dawson among others for contending that expansion of a civilization is an indication of disintegration. They point out, quite properly I think, that expansion also takes place during periods when the nations of a civilization are obviously vital, creative, growing, "healthy." Kroeber adds that inability to expand may in fact contribute to a civilization's decline (Sorokin, *Dynamics*, abridged ed., pp. 565-568; Dawson, *The Dynamics Of World History*, pp. 416-7, pp. 59-60; Kroeber, *Configurations*, p. 691). But even though these criticisms are probably valid, even though expansion is not necessarily an indicator of disintegration, Toynbee is still right in seeing disintegration as a cause of expansion. The break-up of crystalized patterns has provided conditions under which military and other kinds of expansion tend to take place.

4: THE BARBARIAN MENACE

Each civilization applies the concept of barbarians to surrounding peoples. What does this signify?

The concept of the barbarian, of course, originates in the civilized nation. The man outside the civilization is held in contempt or, at best, patronized. He himself acquiesces in this judgment of his inferiority, or fights to overcome it. It is his feelings about his situation that make him a barbarian. If he were not concerned about the civilization or if he regarded it as simply another alien culture, he would be a primitive.

Does the appearance of the barbarian indicate the disintegration of the civilization, or is he going to evolve regardless of the course of its development? To answer this we shall have to ask what changes take place in the relationships between the civilization and the barbarian. In the earlier stages we see the civilization overwhelming primitive cultures. It is difficult to agree with Toynbee that the barbarian is "charmed." But he is firmly ruled. The rule may be exploitative and arbitrary or it may be benevolent and responsible. Most likely it will be some of both. But the members of the civilization have no doubt of their own superiority and of their right to treat barbarians differently from other members of their own civilization: nabobs properly govern Indians; pioneers properly shoot them.

As the relationship between civilization and barbarian progresses, of course it changes. The barbarians become acquainted with the civilization. Some are educated in the civilization itself, or become acquainted with its institutions through serving in its armies or its colonial administration. Those who are most perceptive and who have the most contact with the civilization become dissatisfied. They become desirous of the benefits of the civilization, yet they are never accepted by it. But they have been so transformed that they are no longer able to accept their own culture as it is. In the nineteenth century a term was coined for these unhappy in-betweens: the intelligentsia. An intelligentsia has existed wherever there have been barbarians.

There is also a parallel between the barbarian intelligentsia and the internal intelligentsia: both appear if members of one sub-culture/class regard those of another as less "civilized," and if members of this other acknowledge that a difference exists. The French middle class of the eighteenth century or the American Negroes of the twentieth can be seen as an internal intelligentsia in so far as they are attempting to apply established political and economic techniques to gain equality. The internal intelligentsia may also be charmed by another level of culture in its own civilization, only to find it cannot translate it to the people with whom it originally identified. Then the chances are it will be alienated by this.

It is the members of the intelligentsia who produce changes within a civilization and between the civilization and a primitive culture. An intelligentsia, as Crane Brinton observes, constitutes the white corpuscles of a culture. One always exists. But if it is too large and active, the culture can no longer hold it without disruption.

Eventually the civilization begins to lose control of the barbarian. The desire of the barbarian to manage his own destiny, to be quit of the civilization (but not its ideas), becomes so strong that the civilization, despite great apparent determination, can no longer dominate. Even though it uses elaborate weapons and greater forces in the field, it is unable to wear down or effectively combat mobile barbarian forces that seem to melt away whenever open conflict seems imminent. Sooner or later the barbarian becomes strong enough to win his independence, or the leaders of the civilization, beset with problems that are to them more central, are not willing to continue indefinitely the effort necessary to maintain a tenuous control.

One of the factors that gives the barbarian his victory is his "fanaticism." The term is applied, of course, by the civilized society. It means that the barbarian is willing to go to extremes that the civilized man considers irrational. It means that he is willing to die for values that the civilized man doesn't consider worth the sacrifice. The relationship between this fanaticism and what I have called derivative nationalism is very close: with the latter, the barbarian is fighting for an idea learned from the civilization. The territory he wishes to control was probably defined by the civilization. An arbitrary set of boundary lines established for administrative convenience by the civilized society becomes the sacred territory for which the barbarian gives his life. Whatever he fights for has probably been developed and explained for him by his leaders, themselves members of the intelligentsia, who have acquired their ideas from the civilization they are opposing.

The appearance of the barbarian does not say much in itself about the phase of the civilization's development. The barbarian is likely to be on stage from the time the civilization first begins to expand geographically. A surer sign of disintegration would be the triumph of the barbarian. His victory may be a sign of a loss of will in the civilization. The very concept of fanaticism indicates the complementary development of an attitude akin to the world-weariness of a disintegrating state system. But the way in which the political separation takes place may be important here. Toynbee speaks about a civilization in growth "charming." Well, if the barbarian seeking political separation is amicably granted that separation, and if the civilized government retains economic and cultural relationships with the barbarian, this element of charm remains. The barbarian is free, but he chooses to remain associated with the civilization. The civilization would thus have succeeded in revising its colonial institutions to meet changing conditions.

Barbarians, however, have not always been satisfied with achieving independence from the civilization. They have also frequently conquered and overrun the civilization, the blend sometimes leading to the creation of a new phase of growth. In this sense the barbarians resemble the peripheral areas of the civilization itself. Both learn from the civilization; both expand more freely; and both tend to dominate the mother culture. Where both exist, however, the peripheral power will probably dominate. It has more vitality than the core powers and a superior technology to the barbarian's. Then the peripheral areas are likely to take over the central civilization in the domination or control of the barbarian peoples. Relationships may run fairly smoothly, and some of the charm may return, if the barbarian resentment is reserved for the colonialists of the central area. It is only when peripheral areas have not developed, and disintegration has proceeded for a considerable time, that the barbarian is likely to dominate the civilization itself.

Frequently the barbarian proves an inefficient ruler. The qualities that make a good revolutionary do not necessarily make a good administrator. He must govern without the limitations imposed by the defeated civilization and without the controlling customs that once enabled his culture to function effectively at a primitive level. Living a fluid existence, relatively free from authority, lacking regional attachments and accustomed to appropriating whatever is needed, the barbarian leaders are not trained for maintaining a civilization that requires respect for authority, attachment to locality and acceptance of a law code based on a different concept of number, situation and relationships. The intelligentsia will have some education in the techniques of government, but there are not sufficient cadres under them to manage a modern government, not to speak of transforming an economy. Their difficulty will be compounded by the excessive expectations raised by the defeat of the power that had been blamed for all evils. When the leaders fail to meet expectations, they are likely to be overthrown and replaced by a leadership more irresponsible and less capable. Such cultures are not likely to survive long beyond a primitive level unless they get outside support from a civilization, which is not likely to come from the declining central civilization, but it might if peripheral powers have assumed the leadership of the old central areas. If he accepts this support, the barbarian is threatened with the possibility of falling under a new alien sphere of influence; if he does not he faces the probability of revolution, schism, returning to primitivism: such is the dilemma of the barbarian.

The relevance of the barbarian to Western history is obvious. Russia and the United States are today peripheral areas of European civilization; the "underdeveloped" nations, formerly controlled by the colonial powers, are the mergng barbarians. Their ability to achieve development on their own is sometimes in doubt because of the immense difficulties of raising capital, of gearing the development of factors of production in relation to one another, of controlling population growth, of developing political techniques appropriate to the management of economic problems, including a technique that will enable governments to withhold current production in order to create capital that will serve unborn generations.

The future in the short run belongs to the peripheral nations, whose capital development has come about as the result of a combination of the industrial revolution and Toynbee's law of peripheral domination. The future in the long run may belong to the barbarians, for some day Western civilization might be a core area, as Italy and Europe have been earlier, and by that time some of the barbarian areas may emerge as the civilized peripheral areas of a world civilization. This assumes, however, that the impact of Western civilization will not stimulate new civilizations of an independent character or revive one or more of the older civilizations of Asia. It also assumes that the barbarians have neither been absorbed by other civilizations, nor reverted to primitive levels of culture.

NOTES

a. Barbarians Within a Civilization

The fact that men within a civilization sometimes behave "barbarously," like the Nazis, has nothing to do with the presence of barbarians. While Vandals or Indians may behave in a manner unpleasant to civilized men, their "barbarous" conduct is by no means their monopoly. Barbarians can often be humane and dignified, just as civilized men are often ruthless and uncouth.

b. Barbarian Acquisition of Techniques

In the case of the barbarian, Toynbee seems to be right in suggesting that political techniques precede ideas and aesthetics. But this is not because of deficiencies in the projecting mechanisms of the civilization, it is because the military and political techniques are most relevant to the problems of the barbarian. Yet even at that we must employ ideas and attitudes of the civilization in order to develop a cause to defend with the newly acquired techniques.

c. When the Hordes Don't Appear

If you are living in a civilization overrun by "barbarian hordes" (whether peripheral or primitive) you probably wish you were elsewhere. But as Quigley points out, if a disintegrating civilization is so remote that it is not attacked, its decline is likely to be long and dreary, with ever less hope of reconstitution (*Evolution Of Civilizations*, p. 91).

Sources

A. Transmission Between Civilizations

Spengler, intransferability of culture, *The Decline Of The West*, II: 55-60; Toynbee, "Processes of Radiation and Reception," *A Study Of History*, VIII: 481-521; Sorokin, diffusion and transmissibility, *Social Philosophies Of An Age Of Crisis*, pp. 299-305; congeniality between cultures, *Society, Culture And Personality*, pp. 573-8; Kroeber, diffusion and resistance to it, *Anthropology*, pp. 411-8.

B. Conflict Between Civilizations

Toynbee, "The Drama of Encounters," *Study*, VIII: 454-80; "The Consequences of Encounters," VIII: 522-629; Quigley, destruction of civilizations, *The Evolution of Civilizations*, pp. 91-2; Nikolai Danilevsky, why Europe hates Russia, described by Sorokin, *Social Philosophies*, pp. 69-71; Quincy Wright must deal with the subject of his *Study Of War*, but I don't seem to be able to find it.

C. The Barbarian Menace

Toynbee, "Heroic Ages," *Study*, VIII: 1-77; radiation by charm and by force, V: 198-203. Walter Webb's *The Great Frontier* deals with encounters between civilizations and barbarians in the past five centuries.

VII

THE CIVILIZATION TO END ALL CIVILIZATIONS

1: Is Western Civilization Unique?

If encounters between civilizations muddle the tracing of individual patterns, what are we to say about the effects of the unprecedented expansion of Western civilization? Is it conceivable that the great explorations beginning in the fifteenth century, and the tremendous improvements in transportation and communications that followed, may have stultified attempts to isolate and understand individual cultures at the very time such study was beginning? Could it be that the consequent increased contact between civilizations stimulated the study of comparative history just as it was making such a study obsolescent? Do comparative generalizations about Egypt and Mesopotamia really have any contemporary relevance?

I see two basic questions involved here. First: is Western civilization a new species, in a class by itself, incomparably different from all other civilizations that have ever existed? Second: does its worldwide expansion threaten (or promise) to end the possibility of development for all other civilizations? Not to keep you in suspense, I am going to answer both questions in the negative.

It is clear that Western civilization is vastly different from any other. In its breaking of restraints, in the threat of destruction it has created for itself and the world, in its rate of change and degree of technological development, in its accumulation of knowledge, Western civilization has far outstripped all others. Statistically in thousands of ways it dwarfs all other civilizations combined.

And yet it is clear that any of the other civilizations seemed unique to those who lived in them, and indeed there can be little doubt that each *was* unique. The similarities only emerge from a distance and always with modifications. In terms of form Western civilization seems rather orthodox. It has had a clear-cut feudal period and an orthodox state system. It developed most of the usual patterns of art and philosophy and religion. It may be that it appears even more than usually orthodox because its picture has been painted by its own representatives, and that other civilizations have been somewhat readjusted to fit the Western pattern. But even allowing for error arising from this distorted perspective, in its general contours Western civilization does not appear to be unusual.

What does appear to be unusual is the extent to which those contours have been developed. Whether the quality (or perhaps lack of some quality) that drives Faustian Man to do things with such energy and to carry them so far with so much noise and so much fuss — whether this quality is brand new in the universe, or only something that distinguishes Western man from Classical, it has undoubtedly made a vast difference in the extent of this development. And this quality, combined with his scien-tific-technological bent, has led him to achieve an incredible standard of living, to provide conditions encouraging worldwide reproduction in overwhelming numbers, and to create weapons capable of destroying both the numbers and the standard of living, his and everybody else's. Free-ranging in his survey of other civilizations, Western man has had unique opportunities to profit from the efforts of other men. Indeed, it is asserted that Western man outstrips all others not only in his accumulation of knowledge, but even in his understanding of moral responsibility.

What is the point of comparing such a civilization with what relics we can find of the Hittites?

The answer depends on whether you focus your attention on formation or the consequences of formation, on structure or the development of structure. It is the extent to which the structure of Western civilization has developed as a result of its particular nature that makes it seem unique. The Faustian tendency to penetrate the unknown, which Spengler traces back to the Gothic cathedral, is not in itself the tendency that makes West-ern man so different. We do not find him beyond comparison with classical times in his early modern period. It is rather the harnessing of this Faustian characteristic to machine power that has ignited his transformation. But what is there in this transformation that entitles Faustian man to a special classification? One civilization may be infinitely larger than another, it may have more complicated apparatus, greater speeds and a denser population. But these factors do not measure its essential qualities. Perhaps no one but a Faustian man would suppose that they would. Quantity can never escape the grasp of scientific imagination, or else it would be folly to make maps of Russia or models of the local galaxy.

The improvement and elaboration of techniques is to be expected with the secularization of any civilization. Technology tends to improve despite the fluctuations of other patterns. A pattern of scientific thought can run its course and come to an end, but the technology created out of it remains, and can be improved and refined. It is clear that technology is derivative, that it should not be regarded as a primary criterion for evaluation. It happens that Western technology is far more elaborated, specialized, extended, improved and refined than any other. But it is a technology for all that.

Western man, then, is not uniquely different from all other men who have inhabited the earth. He is different in his spacial and technological conceptions, but comparable to others in the way he develops, and is subject to the same generalizations that concern all civilized men.

NOTES

a. The Perils of Autobiography

Comparative historians seem to have difficulty placing their own civilization in perspective. Since they are writing in response to it, they give the impression that they are really talking about their own culture and their own times, reaching to others for support when the support happens to be available.

Toynbee, on the other hand, is rather coy about discussing the West. Should he not set it aside on the ground that it has not yet run its course and therefore all judgments must be tentative? Won't what we say now look foolish to those who decipher it for the next civilization but one?

In the end, of course, he does discuss it — for pages and pages. For, like it or not, Western civilization happens to be the one we live in. The writer may develop his theories from comparative studies, but he is obliged to apply them to his own culture regardless of the consequences. He may look silly or what he says may be applied, out of context, to causes he does not condone. He cannot do anything about this except develop a very thick skin. If he chooses not to enter the arena, not to apply his understanding to the contemporary world, others less qualified than he will undertake to make the applications for him.

b. The View from the West

As a vantage point, the West seems as good as any. Western man lives in a culture that has followed a normal pattern of development and happens to have within its pattern a strong emphasis on empirical detachment. A comparative historian living in Egypt in the time of the Fifth Dynasty would go far astray if he were to assume he could predict the Egyptian future by finding a pattern in other civilizations, or if he tried to use Egypt as his model for comparison.

And yet, as it happens, it was an Egyptologist, Flinders Petrie, who developed the first modern theory of civilizations, and he did use Egyptian history as a basis. Not only that, but he developed and presented his theory in a little more than a hundred pages. Subsequent comparative historians have had firm footing and a good deal of breathing space compared to Petrie.

c. New World Man vs. Faustian Man

Some writers, like Lewis Mumford and Karl Jaspers (*The Transformations of Man* and *The Origin and Goal of History*) believe that somewhere around the fifteenth century man changed in such a way that he became different from civilized men of all previous periods. This New World Man, as Mumford calls him, was far more unrestrained, materialistic and egalitarian than any of the Old World Men had been.

The qualities that Mumford sees in New World Man are very similar to those Spengler attributes to Faustian man. Thus both Mumford and Spengler see a man uniquely different from all who have ever lived — just as all others have been uniquely different. I think it is the virtue of Spengler, the supposed wild man of comparative history, that he always tried to maintain a balance between the comparative and unique aspects of all cultures.

To insist that a new man exists in all circumstances, or to insist that the man of our culture is no different from men of other cultures — both are equally limiting. Each concept has its applications in specific situations and the applications are not mutually exclusive.

d. Is Technology a Substitute for Creativity?

No. As technology becomes more elaborate, more specialization becomes necessary and men may have less time to develop their total capacities. To this extent technology can contribute to the loss of opportunity to exercise imagination and thus inhibit the development of new creative phases. It is always possible, however, for new creative outbursts to arise out of advanced technologies and even to be inspired by these technologies.

e. An Arm is an Arm

Western civilization may have attained a preposterous level of development beside which all others seem puny and insignificant, but:

At one point Alice grows so large that she fills the White Rabbit's house and must stick her arm out the window in order to fit at all. The following conversation ensues between the rabbit and his gardener outside:

"Now tell me, Pat, what's that in the window?"

"Sure, it's an arm, yer honour!"

"An arm, you goose! Who ever saw one that size? Why it fills the whole window!"

"Sure, it does, yer honour: but it's an arm for all that."

2: Are Civilizations Obsolescent?

But even granting that Western civilization in itself might be comparable to others, what does the logic of its development hold for the future of other civilizations? The possibility that it might by its nature and scope permanently end the world of multiple civilizations has been envisioned in several ways: Western technology may evolve a war so destructive that no civilization can ever again emerge; Western expansion may so engulf the world that no evolving civilization will be able to gain the freedom to articulate itself; Western technology may be adopted by the world, and then, because of its vulnerabilities (specialization and independence), collapse so disastrously that no culture will ever again rise above an agrarian level; Western know-how may effectively solve the problems that have stumped other civilizations heretofore so that a permanently self-renewing world civilization will emerge and all others — the Greek, the European, the Chinese — will appear in retrospect to have been preliminary sketches for a master painting.

If any of these possibilities, dire or hopeful, come into realization, this book becomes an obituary for a 6,000 year flash. Well enough. Obituaries should be written. But I do not think any of these possibilities will be realized.

War techniques, like other techniques, tend to develop cumulatively regardless of the fluctuations of other patterns in a civilization. When a state system becomes enmeshed in a transitional phase, nations are likely to be a good deal less secure and more inclined therefore to allocate resources toward military development. Thus more comes to be spent on the development of war techniques than on anything else and it is the study of war techniques that produces developments in other fields. War is transformed from the derivative to the dominant factor in technological development.

Now war is not necessarily destructive to a civilization. It can serve to destroy institutions that were impeding development and it can stimulate all kinds of activity, creating new economic markets, unifying nations, sanctifying causes, maufacturing heroes, inspiring themes for literature and art. Even an increase in war can continue to have a stimulating effect if the civilization as a whole is growing in size and complexity. But in many civilizations a point is reached in which the emphasis placed on war is such that it begins to have a destructive effect on the fabric of the culture, to contribute to the disintegration of the civilization or to create a receptivity to the imposition of an empire at any cost by any power that can do it.

The larger and more complex a civilization, the larger the war it can absorb, but also the larger the war it is capable of creating. World War II was an immense war, resulting in the deaths of tens of millions of people. But it did stimulate all kinds of activity, it created new economic markets, unified nations, created causes, provided inspiring themes. World War III looks to be a war of the proper proportion to have a disintegrative effect on Western civilization.

If such a war were relatively restricted, it might create such an aversion to war that an empire would be accepted under the rule of any power that still had the will and strength to impose it. Government would probably be authoritarian no matter who controlled it, and survivors would have problems too immediate and desperate to worry about doctrines.

If such a war were more extensive, it might force men to survive as best they were able, wherever they might be. They would have to live from hand to mouth without benefits of the technology to which they were accustomed. Feudal areas would emerge, because enough knowledge would be retained to prevent a return to primitivism. If World War III destroyed Western civilization in this manner it would be necessary to add a footnote on a comparative chart explaining that this particular entity had normal feudal and national periods but lacked an imperial system because of deviations in its patterns of technology.

Compared with the threat of explosive destruction, the threat of smothering seems mild. But comparative historians have been concerned about the effects of a global civilization. Suppose the techniques and approaches of Western man should be adopted the world over? Certainly the product that Western man offers is immediately attractive, and characteristically he has not been modest in offering his way of life to the rest of the world. The greater comfort and leisure that his way promises have been seductive. Leaders of other civilizations who have fought to preserve their own traditions have been replaced time and again by an aggressive intelligentsia that is determined to impose Western methods. The development of Faustian transportation and communication has greatly expedited the transmission of these techniques. (It has also provided a sense of proportion, for despite its size the expanded West is much smaller than the Roman Empire in terms of accessibility.)

But if these techniques do carry a Western style with them, and Western civilization does become a world civilization, what will happen when, sooner or later, this civilization loses its developmental momentum? There must come a moment, says Lewis Mumford, "when all the unknown lands have been explored, when all the arable soils have been put under cultivation, when even the largest city must cease to spread because it has coalesced with a dozen other large cities in a formless mass. . ." (*The Transformation of Man*, p. 116). "What then?" asks Kroeber. If there is "no new culture to take over responsibility and start fresh with new values . . . — what then?" (*Anthropology*, p. 385).

We do not know of course. But it is unlikely that the world will fall into an unbreakable pattern of meaninglessness. It is unlikely that all future civilizations will be stifled by the deadly embrace of a mouldering Western giant.

All civilizations eventually outlive their developmental potential, and this will mean inevitable loss of control of some areas, and the possibility for the development of new civilizations with a minimum of pseudomorphosis. The depth of the Western expansion is open to question. Rather than destroying other civilizations it may well stimulate their revival or, in eliciting countercultural drives, bring about the creation of entirely new civilizations. If these civilizations all have a machine-powered technology, they will bear some resemblance to one another and as a group perhaps be distinguished from the agrarian civilizations of earlier millenniums. But they will still have their patterns of aesthetics, ideas and attitudes. The present cosmopolitan similarity of capital cities throughout the world reflects a combination of Western phase of development, Western communications and Western-barbarian relationships. This set of relationships will change and the superficial cosmopolitan uniformity will disappear in a reaction against its superficiality.

The dangers of technological suicide are foreseen not so much by the comparative historians as by the demographers, ecologists and cyberneticists of our time — an indication, surely, that this is a danger unique in history. Civilizations have been destroyed by war, but never by technology per se. But a Western civilization that surrounds the earth would have to face several frightening challenges arising out of its own being. Population, stimulated by increased living standards and the dispensation of fruits of the science of medicine, may increase at such a rate that food and energy supplies may be inadequate to provide for it. Resources necessary to maintain a giant world technology supporting tens of billions of people might prove to be inadequate. Yet a partial return to agrarian economy might be impossible because of a loss of know-how and the disappearance of the necessary physical capacities for farming. Even if adequate resources were available, would a system that depends on continually increasing investment eventually run out of areas in which to invest? If ever it falters it faces fearful consequences that economists attribute to the acceleration principle and that the world already knows and fears from its experiences between 1929 and 1941.

Or the technological revolution may create unanswerable psychological problems. What will happen when machines and chemistry obviate the necessity for the great majority of mankind to engage in production and reproduction? Will a Huxleyan world, overloaded with Beta and Gamma types, lapse into a pitiful soma-supported quasi-existence? Or might there be a tremendous reaction to the obvious limitations of unending materialism, a transferral of interest in the most gifted minds to aesthetics, philosophy and religion? Could technology, by solving the problems for which it was developed, bring about its own downfall because the great problems now lie in non-material areas? If this technological apparatus were to collapse it would bring a world civilization down with it, and the results could be so prolonged and frightful that nuclear destruction would seem like social euthanasia.

But the technological problem is the kind that Faustian man best understands and is best qualified to meet. If this were the only threat, he could solve such problems indefinitely. He can turn his engineering ingenuity toward the development of synthetic power, the uncovering of new resources, the conservation and replenishment of the old (a major area for investment, by the way), and the reduction of population through safe, effective and possibly mandatory oral contraceptives. The development of methods for producing food without soil, the extensive use of subterranean and ethereal dwellings, and the colonization of other planets might not even be necessary. But if these expedients were necessary, they would probably be developed.

The end of Western civilization would more likely come about because the Faustian materialistic spirit has run its pattern and Faustian man has turned his attention to the exploration of the spiritual world (which, after all, promises the most unreachable unknowns). But even so, representatives of some other newer civilization might be ready to run the world technology and unwilling to allow its collapse.

And should this technological collapse occur, and should civilization fall irreparably back to the agrarian level, new civilizations might still arise, even though they might not be capable of machine-powered industrial revolutions. In that case future historians would say that the machine-powered industrial revolution was an anomalous aspect of Western civilization. The post-industrial agrarian civilizations would develop in their own ways, solve their own problems, and create their own patterns of meaningful art, government, religion and philosophy.

The three possibilities considered thus far envision the destruction of a capacity to produce new civilizations. Another possibility — the creation of a harmonious, perpetually self-adjusting world civilization — would end the necessity to produce further civilizations.

If knowledge could be weighed, there is little doubt that there is more of it in Western civilization. We know more about the nature of the universe and can therefore substitute empirically tested facts for philosophical speculation. Not only does Western civilization have more knowledge, perhaps, than all the other civilizations put together, but it has printing and electronic means of communication that make this knowledge more accessible to more people. Might we not reach a level of understanding of the workings of civiliation, and of the nature of man, such that we can perpetually reconstitute a world civilization? Might not the very formidability of the other threats to civilization provide the needed incentive to enable civilized man to direct his capacities toward the creation and maintenance of such a civilization?

Perhaps. But has the accumulation of knowledge really progressed so far? For knowledge, like technology, must be considered in relation to the civilization that has acquired it. A large civilization requires more knowledge to function at all. The men within the civilization, however, are still men with the same limitations and capacities that control men of other cultures. Therefore, if they diligently apply themselves, they can learn more about any particular subject than was known in any other civilization, but they can do this only at the cost of sacrificing knowledge of all the other subjects. And if, like our comparative historians, they seek to understand greater areas of subject matter, they leave themselves open to the charge of lacking depth. For the individual the possibilities of acquiring knowledge have not changed all that much. For the civilization there remains a proportion between size, complexity and knowledge.

Nor is there any guarantee that knowledge will continue to grow. Educational techniques in the West have for some time challenged the accumulation of knowledge for its own sake and have stressed instead the development of the capacity to think. Thus future generations may possess less knowledge than their ancestors. Also more and more courses are being added to school and college curricula. Therefore, future generations may have to choose between being broadly and shallowly educated or specializing in narrower and narrower areas. Either choice would lead to a loss of "basic" knowledge. Not only may knowledge be lost, but it may become less desirable. If it becomes more difficult to obtain, and that which is acquired fails to solve frustrating problems or only adds to frustration, the desire for knowledge may be further subordinated to desire for power, money, leisure, or faith.

But even if the degree of knowledge to maintain a world civilization could be acquired, and even if a capacity to maintain it existed, such a civilization would break down from the same internal processes that have ended and will always end all cultures.

To recapitulate: Western civilization does not appear to be a different species of culture and the possibility of its worldwide expansion does not seem likely to prevent the development of other civilizations.

Even if Western civilization were clearly different from other civilizations, and even if it did seem likely to exterminate all rivals, the study of civilizations would be worthwhile. We would be much poorer than we are now if we limited our pursuits to those subjects that have demonstrated contemporary relevance. But it also happens, in this case, that the study of comparative history does have contemporary relevance. Indeed, the more basic a study is, the more it aims at underlying processes and origins, the more contemporary relevance it is likely to have. Judging the West by comparative criteria is likely to be both more logical and more fruitful than treating it always as a novelty.   (See SOURCES, A).

NOTES

a.   War and Heavy Industry

The relation between the development of technology and that of war may be illustrated by the modern connotations attached to the term "heavy industry." For heavy industry refers to the production of capital equipment which is a necessary base for the development of mass-produced consumer goods. It is also necessary, of course, for the construction of implements of war. But so important has war become that to favor the development of heavy industry has come to mean favoring a military economy and therefore opposition to production for the sake of immediate consumption.

b.   The Destruction of Mankind

We can soberly consider the destruction of civilizations against past experiences. But the destruction of mankind is simply ludicrous. It is amusing beause it is incongruous. "You might think it's funny now," a student declared angrily, "but you won't think it's so funny after it happens."

c.   Hellenic vs. Western Expansion

Toynbee thinks the expansion of the modern West is comparable to expansion in the Hellenistic age. By his count Alexander the Great and his epigoni encountered more civilizations than the West has encountered (A Study of History, VIII: 404). This assumes, however, that we ignore the extent of the respective impacts, and accept Toynbee's delineations of civilizations, along with a kind of one-civilization, one-vote, principle.

d. The Source of Future Civilizations

If Western civilization blankets the world, where will future civilizations come from? Toynbee looks to Africa which (outside of Egypt) seems to be virgin territory. It may be an advantage to be free of the incubus of previous civilizations, but I think that new civilizations can start anywhere. If Africa has the advantage of freer possibilities for development, Asia has the advantage of strongly established patterns that could be used in different ways, just as the West drew strongly on classical and Magian motifs. One thing the study of past civilizations has taught us is that they frequently begin in unexpected and unhospitable places. The next one, therefore, will probably have its origins in the Antarctic or Boston or some place like that.

3: Does History Have a Pattern?

The spread of Western technology seems to be a unique event. It is often said that the present era of science and technology is as different from the prescientific civilizations as those civilizations were different from prehistorical cultures.

Might it be, then, that there are patterns of relationships to be discerned outside of civilizations as well as inside them? Might it be that the encounters we have been calling "fortuitous" actually have a logic of their own?

There is a striking similarity among many of the ancient civilizations. The first four were agrarian, river cultures. Subsequent and derivative civilizations, though they did not begin on rivers, were comparable in form.

Students of comparative history and comparative religion have distinguished a period of unusual philosophical fermentation in the first millennium B.C. Karl Jaspers and Lewis Mumford have called this the "Axial Period." It was a period of amazing intellectual fermentation, of the appearance of the most seminal philosophers of all time in China, India, the Middle East and Greece. Men for the first time began to rely on their own thinking as individuals and to develop some remarkable solutions to problems of good and evil. While civilizations continued their individual processes of development, a new element was added which all have found congenial at certain phases of their development.

The present millenium has added not only a world technology, but a reliance on the empirical method. From now on, unless there is a tremendous break with the past, men will test ideas they have developed through reason and intuition against natural or experimental data.

Thus, while individual civilizations have continued to follow partially recurrent patterns of development, there has been an accumulation of method and content to be employed as each successive civilization reaches a self-conscious, rational, empirical phase.

The fact that civilizations themselves have existed for a relatively short period suggests that they may be part of a larger developmental pattern, that they may have been created by men to meet certain problems and may, as a category, be replaced as the problems change. This has already been suggested by Flinders Petrie, who sees progress in the long term changing the nature of civilizations; by Toynbee who looks for higher forms than civilizations; by Mumford, who sees the day of comparable civilizations as already past; by Sorokin, who says civilizations never existed in the first place; and by Kroeber, who suggests that the civilizations concept may not be the final explanation for cultural macrodynamics.

This is possible. But man, as long as he lives, will live in some pattern of relationship. Long after the civilization flourished, the primitive culture continued to exist. Some more appropriate relationship may similarly supercede the civilization, or outlast it. But so long as man remains what he is, he will live in some pattern of relationships, and these patterns will not be unrecognizably different from those that have already existed many times.

So long as man remains what he is. But will he? I have assumed the nature of man is relatively constant. This may be an error.

Downing Bowler suggests that psychoanalysis is today where physiology was in the seventeenth century. We are learning a tremendous amount about the nature of man and are only approaching the point at which we can begin to do something about it. Just as the seventeenth-century discoveries of Harvey and Borelli have led to remarkable changes in the propensity for man to survive, so the discoveries of the twentieth century may lead to remarkable changes in the way in which man acts. And if the understanding of the nature of man does bring about a radical reorientation in his behavior, a change may take place that is no less momentous than that brought about by the agricultural revolution that preceded the origin of civilizations. In that event the chances for a vital, happy world culture of the future may increase considerably.

But even supermen must live in some kind of pattern of relationships, and this pattern will still have a great deal to do with the realization of their possibilities.

It appears, then, that there may be patterns that include all civilizations and all mankind and all history. Just as civilizations can include complete cultures, so the great patterns of history include civilizations. We don't understand them very well, and perhaps we have too little data to work with, but the continued study of civilizations as a whole will also contribute to our understanding of these supercivilizational patterns.

NOTES

a. The East-West Pattern

Another supercivilizational pattern shared by Petrie, Toynbee and a number of Orientalists envisions all the Eastern civilizations as being more like one another and less like the Mediterranean and Western civilizations. Petrie and Toynbee have observed a give-and-take relationship between the two great world regions in which first one and then the other dominates. Petrie attributes this to differences in phase of development, Toynbee to successive responses to challenges. Jaspers, on the other hand, warns against accepting a "Mother Asia" concept. China and India, he insists, have differentiated themselves from the Asian past as much as Europe has.

I think there may be several important supercivilizational patterns of this kind. Different supercivilizational patterns can exist at the same time, just as regional characteristics can exist within a civilization or a nation.

b. Systems are Systems of Systems

So Bowler observes. Social systems are limited by definition. There is nothing beyond a world system of civilizations . There is nothing beyond the individual who composes the simplest society. But that individual, of course, is a system in biological if not historical terms. And the cells of which that individual is composed can be broken down into further components. The world civilization intimately relates to the biological system that supports it and to the systems of earth and atmosphere that support them, and they in turn are related to the systems of the universe.

There is no basic entity.

There is no ultimate relationship.

c. The Denial of Historical Patterns

The denial of historical patterns manifested by historians like H.A.L. Fisher and Pieter Geyl as well as philosophers like R. G. Collingwood and Karl Popper is usually focused primarily and most usefully on determinism. Certainly there are no inevitable patterns. But when a Fisher chooses to write about a Macrocosmic Europe or a Geyl about a Microcosmic Netherlands, each must make some important structural choices. He must decide what to exclude and what to emphasize, and he does so on the basis of what he thinks is most important, and that depends on his view of a totally related structure. If Europe has no patterns, if it is only the western-most peninsula of Asia, why should it receive any more consideration as a historical unit than the eastern-most peninsula, which is just as clearly delineated by the Sea of Okhotsk, the Bering Sea, the Arctic Ocean and the Lena River?

4: Does the Past Have a Future?

I have said what I can at present about the nature and interaction of civilizations. I have tried to draw a fuzzy subject with relatively sharp lines. I hope that it will help clarify some conceptions and that it will raise questions about others. I will be pleased if it encourages some historians to stretch themselves a bit more, to try their craftsmanship on the study of history and philosophy of history. I will be even more pleased if it encourages a few students to turn their attention in this direction, to prepare themselves for macrocultural studies, to specialize, that is, in generalization.

There is much to be done. Students of comparative history must sharpen the primitive tools of their trade by developing ways of enlarging their capacity for absorption, correlation and understanding, and by establishing some general order in their field, some measure of agreement on delineation and terminology, some recognition that regardless of whether they call themselves historians, anthropologists, sociologists or philosophers, they are working toward similar objectives; they must also pay more attention to criticizing and correcting their own work and that of their fellow writers; they must apply the principles they have established to particular problems in order to indicate which lines of study should be further pursued, to modify their hypotheses, and to demonstrate that comparative history provides a valid approach to social science; and while they are refining, criticizing and applying their methods, they must continue to produce fresh general comparative studies, for these are likely to become more valuable and reliable as methods improve, criticism corrects and application clarifies.

Admirable as the works so far produced have been, there is reason to hope that better comparative history is still to come. Supposing it were to become more widely understood, and supposing that it were to inspire a large number of teachers to direct their students' attention to the relationships of their various subjects of study and to the relationships of history to other histories, how much better prepared these students might be when they set about unraveling specific problems, how much greater insight coming generations might have. If students in these generations began to consider these broad relationships early on, and if their conjectures were developed in an atmosphere of receptive minds — an advantage not possessed by the Spenglers and Toynbees and Sorokins — who can guess how far they may carry the study of comparative history?

For here, in a society in which many styles are being criticized and shattered, is a swelling style, a fresh, exciting, growing pattern of social study. Its shaping has only just begun.

Notes

a. The Future Study and Teaching of Economics

One of Marx's most important contributions to economic theory was to point out the relation between modes of production and the nature of a society. Comparative history has modified Marx to the extent that we no longer believe that modes of production determine the nature of culture; we believe rather that production and culture change in relation to each other. It is the nature of culture and the nature of change, not production or government or great men, that provides the key to understanding history.

But twentieth-century economists are less historically oriented thn those of the nineteenth century. The study of economics today begins with the study of the modern system in one's own country. And the emphasis seems to be moving from analysis to prescription — students are taught what the incumbent government ought to do about problems almost as soon as they are introduced to the problems themselves. And the text-book publishers vie with one another to produce new editions capable of dealing with the latest problems, preferably problems anticipated in the next few years.

Clearly the economics teachers are out of date. They can put out loose leaf text-books if they like, and send us substitute pages daily, and they will be all the more out of date. For the twentieth century has given us tremendous advantages in viewpoint, and one of the lessons of this viewpoint is that to be up-to-date and in-the-know is to be caught in a megalopolitan, fashion-conscious, superficial atmosphere. The very fact that books do not stand up, that new editions must be written, that libraries are full of editions already outdated, should tell their authors that.

Economists should be concerned first and foremost with methods of production and distribution. (Ever since Mill suggested that distribution was a political rather than an economic problem it has tended to be a theoretical orphan and a pragmatic key to power.) To understand these they should comb history for what it has to tell us about these processes and about their relation to the civilizations or cultures in which they exist. The economic policy of a single contemporary government might be an advanced and rather specialized branch of economics, but it should certainly not be introductory subject matter.

b. The Future Study and Teaching of Government

The last time I attended a convention of the American Political Science Association I was struck by the attention given to the province of political scientists. They were to be careful not to be historians or economists or anthropologists. Jurisdictional overlapping was considered sloppy and unprofessional if not positively immoral.

It is not surprising, therefore, that the study of government can too easily become restricted to a concern with relationships between institutions. The student of government concentrates on how the governmental system is supposed to work. If he is historically oriented he may then show how it evolved. If he is inclined to probe more deeply, he may speculate about the relationships between the political form and the economic system and society. Thus a study of British government will show how the system works, how a law is passed for instance; then how the system evolved from the Glorious Revolution through the nineteenth-century reforms; and finally how these changes reflected the growth of urban power and the industrial revolution. Primarily, however, attention is given to the workings of contemporary government at all levels. Who are the men who really make the decisions now, and how do they arrive at them? How much say did the voter have in the last election and who manipulated him? How do you get your way in the world today?

It is natural, therefore, for teachers of politics (as it is for teachers of economics) to supplement their courses with news magazines, to spend hours of their own valuable time reading contemporary serious papers and journals, and even for schools to make "current events" a separate part of the curriculum. In so doing they engulf themselves in the world of news agencies, who keep their stories constantly "updated" (the word itself is singularly appropriate for the attitude it reflects) by substituting "new leads" whenever anything new happens so that their newspaper clients (who put out several editions daily) can always present the latest; of radio and television stations, which revise news broadcasts hourly, placing primary emphasis on whatever happened most recently. One would expect, however, that an academic world would exist precisely to pursue an alternative to this, to look beyond and through it, to try to understand the jumble of developing patterns from a more detached perspective.

Political scientists and teachers of politics should be concerned first and foremost with methods of political organizations and their relation to the civilizations or cultures in which they exist. The political policy of a single dynasty or administration might be a matter of concern to specialists, but, as with the economic policy of a single government, it should certainly not be introductory subject matter. And the news of the day should be interpreted when relevant as illustrative material, not as the central subject of study. Where history is incorporated it should not be considered as background to be slogged through in order to acquire weapons with which to battle problems of the day. History should show the place that government has in society, the changes that it tends to undergo, and the impermanence to which any form, including the present, is inclined to be subjected.

There is a relevant debate going on in education. One side emphasizes the need to present an understanding of the culture in which one lives. The other emphasizes the need to provide mthods and incentives by which the student will make learning a lifetime project. The up-to-the-minute approach accomplishes neither end: it fails to provide an understanding of the relation of politics or economics to one's own culture (not to mention other cultures) and it fails to provide the methods and incentives with which a student can go on and develop in knowledge, wisdom and understanding.

c.   The Future Study and Teaching of International Relations

International Relations in America is considered a branch of political science. The scope of its study is frequently indicated by the substitution of the term World Politics, and discussion is frequently concerned with the primacy of political or economic forces in determining international decisions. Or else the subject is treated under the title Foreign Policy in which case the political scientist tries to determine what a country — usually the one he happens to live in — should do under certain circumstances. In England the study of international relations is usually considered a branch of history, in which case the student concerns himself with what diplomats have done in the past. Again, the diplomats usually come from his own country.

Today the student of international relations should be concerned with the basic nature of this relationship. He ought to take advantage of the broader view the comparative historians have opened up for him. He certainly ought to realize that even comparative study involves more than the juxtaposition of institutions and economic systems. The state system is an elaborate and total form of relationship that must be explored in relation to government, economic development, and the culture as a whole. A state system must be seen historically, as a developing entity, and comparatively, as one of many such systems that have come into existence.

d.   The Future Study and Teaching of History

The emphasis on politics and economics will probably continue to be valid in the study, teaching and writing of history. After all, history is made through changing political and economic forms. Intellectual and ideological development affects political history and aesthetic development reflects it, but history is made in political and economic change. That is why primitive societies have no history.

But the relation of politics and economics to the patterns of civilization should be more fully explored. If you want to understand history in the twentieth century, you must grasp the macrocultural patterns. No understanding of the details of personalities or institutions or sequence will serve as an adequate substitute. History in the twentieth century cannot be written or taught as if sociology and anthropology did not exist. The student of history has to be aware of the relationship of the culture he is studying to the concentric circles of culture around it, including that of the civilization as a whole.

In trying to understand and interpret all this, the narrative historian is going to make mistakes, and he is going to be exposed to the same kind of ridicule that has greeted the comparative historian. The only way he can avoid error is to limit himself to a very narrow area and learn all there is to know about it. Then he can write history that is nearly perfect. It will be nearly perfect, but it will not be worth reading because he won't understand his subject as well as the historian with a broader view. He will have all the parts, but he won't understand the deeper relationships. The twentieth-century historian who does not attempt to perceive the underlying relationships of culture patterns simply has not discharged the responsibility he has undertaken. The twentieth-century teacher who does not attempt to understand these broader relationships fails his students. In observation as in action you have to make use of the means that are at your command. You have to live in the century in which you live.

e.   The Future of Comparative History

The writing of comparative history presents major difficulties. It cannot be taught at the undergraduate level, so the writer cannot reinforce or test his work in his teaching. Beyond this it is difficult for any one person to acquire an adequate general knowledge of several civilizations, let alone a detailed comparative knowledge of any one phenomenon common to all of them. Toynbee has attempted to get around this difficulty by submitting parts of his manuscript to specialists for comment. Sorokin has been able to employ teams of students to tabulate and perform basic research that no one man could ever have undertaken. Coulborn's conclusions on feudalism were based on a remarkable cooperative enterprise undertaken by a loosely federated team of experts and generalists. The logistics of that operation, which incidently included Kroeber and Toynbee, must have been incredible.

Committees and teams have greater scope than individuals. But they have bureaucratic limitations. Both Sorokin and Coulborn are much more stimulating writers when they are not inhibited by the team data or committee will. The lone wolf will blunder, but his mistakes will be weeded out by time and the criticisms of specialists. A thick skin is probably a helpful asset to the comparative historian, but not if it prevents him from modifying his image when the evidence warrants.

Where are the comparative historians to be found? Coulborn's untimely death denied him the opportunity to write what could have been the most anthropologically-oriented approach since

Kroeber's *Configurations*. For Coulborn was more interested than Kroeber in origins and better grounded in history. Quigley possesses a rare combination of abilities. He writes with knowledge, penetrating judgment and a clear style punctuated with captivating analogies. He is particularly well grounded, as most comparative historians have not been, in economic history and theory. If he is not diverted into too many other seductive areas of interest, he is bound to make a major contribution to the understanding of civilizations. There are other students of social sciences whose interests are turning in this direction. Michael Grant, Frank Manuel, Kenneth Boulding, S.N. Eisenstadt, Cyril Black, Robert Adams and Robert Wesson come to mind. (A committee could think of many more.) Their difficulties are formidable because they do not have much contact with one another, inhibited as they are by the barriers of segregated disciplines. They must also fight or circumvent the establishments that dominate the professional associations and that insist on limiting their explorations to territories that are soft, approved, respectable, and so intensely cultivated that they are bound to yield disappointing results no matter how much genius is applied to them.

What will the comparative historians write? Off the top of my head I can think of a number of promising titles that lack only books to go with them:

Materialism: the study of fluctuations in attitude toward the acquisition of goods and services.

Barbarians: a study of the peoples whose lives were uprooted by encroching civilizations.

Formlessness: a study of the recurrent destruction or loss of form and the conditions that brought it about.

The World Losers: an inquiry into the conditions surrounding the men who thought they could conquer the world, and almost did, but ultimately failed.

Total Wars: how often have they occurred? What has been their effect? Have they had a common cause?

No More Children: a study of the times and situations in which people have wanted to reduce the size of their families or even destroy their own babies.

What is Funny?: a study of the relation of humor and culture.

The Cosmopolitan: a study of the recurrent emergence of the world citizen.

Good Boys and Girls: a comparative study of fluctuating standards of morality in world history.

It is best to stop. The titles seem to be taking a popular turn. Such studies as these should always be done on a genuinely comparative basis, not, as in the past, as a series of random selections from Western history with a polite nod at Greece and Rome. And they should be systematic, with a model of approach preceding actual research.

The pursuit of these studies of particular categories should not impede the development of total theories, for many of the students of particular areas are bound to be motivated to understand the whole.

SOURCES

A. TOYNBEE'S WEST

Toynbee has been most prolific on the subject, though he tends to apologise for writing about it at all. In addition to two short books, *The Prospects of the West* and *Civilization On Trial,* he has given the subject copious treatment in his *Study,* IX: 406-645 with reconsiderations in XII: Ch. XVI.

Others who have dealt with the subject extensively are Kroeber, in *Configurations of Culture Growth,* pp. 699-760; Quigley, *The Evolution of Civilizations,* pp. 210-265; and Clough, *The Rise and Fall of Civilization,* pp. 163-216.

B. IS WESTERN CIVILIZATION UNIQUE?

The basic difference of opinion may be seen by contrasting the view of Karl Jaspers and Lewis Mumford, that Western man is new and unique, to that of Spengler, who sees him as unique only in the sense that each civilization produces its unique qualities. Spengler, *The Decline of the West,* I: Ch. VI, The Faustian Soul; Jaspers, *The Origin and Goal of History,* Part 1: Ch. VI; Mumford, *The Transformations of Man,* Ch. VI, "New World Man."

Unprecented changes in the West: Quincy Wright, *A Study of War,* I: 166-9; Toynbee, *Study,* IX: 465-473.

Technology: Jaspers, *Origin,* pp. 100-125; technology and war: Toynbee, *Study,* abridged ed., I: 192-5; Wright, *A Study of War,* I: 374-7.

C. ARE CIVILIZATIONS OBSOLESCENT?

The danger of one civilization stifling all others: A.L. Kroeber, *Configurations of Culture Growth,* pp. 621-3; *Anthropology,* pp. 384-5; pseudomorphosis: Spengler, *The Decline of the West,* I: 207-214; Schweitzer, *The Decay and the Restoration of Civilization,* pp. 63-4; comparison of Hellenistic and Western dominations of other civilizations: Toynbee, *Study*, VIII: 403-7.

Capacity of Western civilization to solve its problems: Harrison Brown, *The Challenge of Man's Future*, Ch. VII, "Patterns of the Future."

d.   DOES HISTORY HAVE A PATTERN?

This is basically the subject of Jaspers' *Origin* and Mumford's *Transformations*, cited above. But see particularly Jaspers' Part I, Ch. II: "Scheme of World History," showing the modern period as a third major breakthrough in an otherwise cyclical history.

Toynbee has relegated civilizations to a lesser role. See his discussion of churches as "higher species," *Study*, VII: 420-449.

e.   DOES THE PAST HAVE A FUTURE?

Comparative historians on comparative history: Sorokin, *Social Philosophies of an Age of Crisis;* Kroeber, *Style and Civilizations*, Chs. 4 & 5 and Appendix III.

BIBLIOGRAPHY

1: ALPHABETICAL LISTING

I have listed below in alphabetical order those English language books and articles that seem most relevant to an understanding of the nature of civilizations. The reader who wants to pursue a particular subject further should first consult the sources at the end of relevant chapters, and then look further to section two of this bibliography, where the books are listed according to topic.

In several instances I have included books (indicated by asterisks) that look to be relevant, but that I have not seen. The comments on these are based on reviews or conversations.

Adams, Brooks, *The Law of Civilization and Decay*, London, 1903, reprinted in Vintage paperback, 1955; o.p. A curiosity. That it should be revived in paperback is even more curious.

Adams, Henry, *The Degradation of the Democratic Dogma*, New York, Peter Smith, 1949. Both this book and the above are perhaps of more interest to students of Adamses than to students of civilization.

Adams, Robert McC., *The Evolution of Urban Society*, Chicago, Aldine, 1966. A comparison of early Mesopotamian and Mexican societies. The author is cognizant of comparative theory, and its relation or irrelevance to specific problems.

Allen, Philip J., editor, *Pitirim A. Sorokin in Review*, Durham, Duke University Press, 1963. A mild workout by generally friendly critics. Sorokin "replies," understandably, by praising their "admirable understanding, objectivity and elegance."

Anderle, Othmar F., *The Problems of Civilizations*, The Hague, Mouton & Co., 1964.* A report on a conference on the comparative study of civilizations, attended by Sorokin, Kroeber and Coulborn, at Salzburg in 1961.

Bagby, Philip, *Culture and History*, London, Longmans, Green & Co., 1958. More a statement of what needs to be done than a significant contribution in itself.

——"Culture and the Causes of Culture," *American Anthropologist*, LV: 535-554. Among other things, a defense of the "reality" of civilizations.

Barraclough, Geoffrey, *History in a Changing World*, Oxford, Blackwell, 1955. Perceives some of the contributions comparative history can make to narrative history.

Becker, Howard, *Man in Reciprocity*, New York, Praeger, 1956.* A transcript of classroom lectures containing a typology of cultural supersystems on a sacred-secular continuum.

Benedict, Ruth, *Patterns of Culture*, Boston, Houghton Mifflin, 1934; Mentor paperback, 1956. Applies the integration and characterization concepts to primitive cultures. The question is whether such methods can be applied to whole civilizations.

Berdyaev, Nikolai, *The Meaning of History*, London, Geoffrey Bles, 1936. A profound and interesting Russian religious and political philosopher. In one sense the successor of Danilevsky, in another the Russian contemporary of Dawson and Schweitzer.

Bertalanffy, Ludwig von, *General System Theory*, New York, Braziller, 1968. Views comparative history as one of many systems approaches being undertaken simultaneously in mathematics, sciences, philosophy, social sciences and aesthetics.

Beus, J. G. de, *The Future of the West*, London, Eyre & Spottiswoode, 1953. This raised some interesting questions for me when I read it a decade ago. Now it seems rather superficial and derivative.

Black, C. E., *The Dynamics of Modernization*, New York, Harper & Row, 1966; Torch paperback, 1967. Uses comparative method and world scope on a modern historical problem. Black is skeptical about the usefulness of comparing modern problems with those of the distant past.

Bodin, Jean, *Method for the Easy Comprehension of History*, New York, Columbia University Press, 1945; translated by Beatrice Reynolds. Bodin is probably the first Western writer to grasp the possibilities of comparative history.

Boulding, Kenneth, *The Image*, University of Michigan Press, Ann Arbor paperback, 1963. The explanation of the image undertaken here would apply to the model sketched in this book. Boulding's study is also useful in its appraisal of the integrative approach to various disciplines.

——*The Meaning of the Twentieth Century*, New York, Harper and Row; Torch paperback, 1964. Sees recent developments as marking the end of the period of comparable civilizations.

Bowler, T. Downing, *Being and Relatedness*, Bradford, Mass., unpublished multilith, 1959-69; distributed by Bradford Junior College bookstore. Demonstrates a number of insights that can be derived from syncretistic approaches to philosophy, science, psychology, anthropology and comparative religion.

Bozeman, Adda B., *Politics and Culture in International History*, Princeton University Press, 1960; also Princeton U.P. paperback, 1960. A study of international relations in several civilizations. Comparisons and generalizations are mostly left to the reader.

Brinton, Crane, *The Anatomy of Revolution*, New York, Random House, Vintage paperback, 1957; also revised ed. 1967. An example of an effective comparative study undertaken with carefully prescribed limitations within a single civilization.

Brown, Harrison, *The Challenge of Man's Future*, New York, Viking Press paperback, 1954. Raises problems for Western civilization that no other civilization has had to face.

Burckhardt, Jacob, *Force and Freedom*, New York, Pantheon, 1943, 1964; Beacon Press, paperback, 1964; translated by M. D. Hottinger-Mackie, edited by James Hastings Nichols. Really an arrangement of lecture notes, but all the same an interesting example of effective use of the comparative approach in the nineteenth century.

Clough, Shepard B., *The Rise and Fall of Civilization*, London, Skeffington, 1953; Columbia, paperback, 1961. Challenges the thesis that material well-being is an indication of disintegration.

Collingwood, R. G., *The Idea of History*, Oxford, Cumberlege, 1946, also paperback. Early and persistent critic of Toynbee and deterministic history.

Coulborn, Rushton, and others, *Feudalism in History*, Princeton University Press, 1956. An interesting example of committee work, with its advantages of scope and accuracy and its disadvantage of over-elaboration and lack of incisiveness.

Coulborn, Rushton, *The Origin of Civilized Societies,* Princeton University Press, 1959, revised ed., paperback, 1969. Sophisticated in delineation, a model study combining strong background in anthropology with superior knowledge of Eastern civilizations. Cf. the revolution described here with that described by Boulding in *Twentieth Century.*

——"Structure and Process in the Rise and Fall of Civilized Societies," *Comparative Studies in Society and History,* VIII: 404-431, 1966. Coulborn modifies some earlier theories, delineates the basic civilizations, and carries his views beyound the feudal period.

——"The Rise and Fall of Civilizations," *Ethics,* LXIV: 205-216. Compares the approach of the Egyptologist John Wilson with that of Toynbee and Kroeber in the study of the anomalous Egyptian civilization.

——"Survival of the Fittest in the Atomic Age," *Ethics,* LVII: 235-258. Compares basic problem of the nuclear age with that which faced founders of the first civilizations.

——"Toynbee's Reconsiderations: A Commentary," *Journal of World History,* VIII, No. 1, 1964, 15-53. Fair to Toynbee and a contribution to comparative history in itself.

——"A Paradigm for Comparative History?" *Current Anthropology,* Vol. 10, No. 2-3, April-June 1969, 175-178. The prospects for the study of comparative history, sketched by Coulborn a few months before his death in April, 1968.

Coulborn, Rushton and W.E.B. Du Bois, "Mr. Sorokin's Systems," *The Journal of Modern History,* December, 1942, 500-521. This rather surprising combination of scholars (Coulborn and Du Bois were professors of history, and sociology respectively at Atlanta University in the early 1940's — just after Sorokin's fourth volume came out) has produced the most cogent appraisal of Sorokin's basic theory and its relation to that of Spengler and Toynbee.

Coulborn, Rushton and Joseph R. Strayer, "The State and Religion: An Exploratory Comparison in Different Cultures," *Comparative Studies in Society and History,* October 1958, 38-57. A comparison of the relation between government and religion in six civilizations.

Cowell, Frank R., *History, Civilization and Culture,* London, Black, 1952, o.p.; Boston, Beacon Press, 1952, o.p. An adulatory introduction to Sorokin's theories.

——*Values in Human Societies,* Boston, Porter Sargent, 1969.* A fuller exposition of Sorokin's life and work, scheduled for publication this fall.

Croce, Benedetto, *The Philosophy of Giambattista Vico,* London, Latimer, 1913; translated by R.G. Collingwood. Croce's interpretation is more relevant than Vico's writing.

Dawson, Christopher, *The Dynamics of World History,* London, Sheed and Ward, 1957; Mentor paperback, 1962; ed. by John J. Mulloy. A useful arrangement of Dawson's work together with a summary that underlines his basic theories.

——*Enquiries into Religion and Culture,* London, Sheed and Ward, 1933. Contains an early essay on cycles of history written by Dawson before he had read Spengler or Toynbee.

——*Religion and Culture,* London, Sheed and Ward, 1948; Meridian paperback. Emphasizes crucial role of religion in determining the nature of a civilization.

Eisenstadt, S.N., *The Political System of Empires,* Glencoe, The Free Press, 1963. Logically constructed, closely argued, strongly supported, difficult. Useful hypothese for specific studies on economics, political structure, or class.

Eisenstadt, S.N., ed., *The Decline of Empires,* Englewood Cliffs, Prentice-Hall, 1967; also Prentice-Hall paperback, 1967. More about total process than decline. Except for a few leading comments by the editor, most of the comparisons are left to the reader.

Erwin, Robert, "Civilization as a Phase of World History," *The American Historical Review,* July 1966, 1181-1198. Argues that civilizations have perished because of external attack, not internal decline.

Frankel, Charles, *The Case for Modern Man,* London, Macmillan, 1957; Beacon paperback, 1959. A spirited reply to the gloom-and-doom aspects of comparative history.

Geyl, Pieter, *Debates with Historians,* Groningen, Wolters, 1955; Meridian paperback. An amusing and effective critic of of Toynbee and Sorokin.

Gottschalk, Louis, ed., *Generalization in the Writing of History,* University of Chicago Press, 1963.* Classifies kinds of history written, concentrates mostly on comparative history and philosophy of history.

Grant, Michael, *Ancient History*, London, Methuen, 1952; Harper, Torch paperback. A comparative study of ancient societies, with analytical chapters devoted to war, state systems, nationalism, social structure, leadership and war. Didactic and cautious, but refreshingly hostile to the Ancients.

Herskovits, Melville, *Man and His Works*, New York, Knopf, 1956. Deals with structure and dynamics of culture. Rich in example, difficult to skim without reading.

Hughes, H. Stuart, *Oswald Spengler: A Critical Estimate*, New York, Scribner's, 1952. Fair, perceptive, considers relationship between Spengler and his more important predecessors and successors.

Ibn Khaldun, *The Muquaddimah*, London, Routledge and Kegan Paul, 1958; New York, Pantheon, 1958, three volumes; translated by Franz Rosenthal. A comparative history from another time and another world.

Jaspers, Karl, *The Origin and Goal of History*, New Haven, Yale University Press, 1953; translated by Michael Bullock. An attempt to reconcile world history with comparative history. Cf. Mumford's *Transformations*.

Kann, Robert A., *The Problem of Restoration*, Berkeley, University of California Press, 1968. A comparative study of twelve situations in which political stability was restored after a revolution. Examples drawn from European and ancient history.

Kluckhohn, Clyde, "The Concept of Culture" in *Culture and Behavior*, Glencoe, The Free Press, 1962, paperback, pp. 19-73. An imaginary conversation between members of various professions trying to establish what they mean by "culture."

Koneczny, Feliks, *On the Plurality of Civilizations*, London, Polonica Publications, Series No. 2, 1962.* Preface by Arnold Toynbee. An apparently controversial comparative history by a Polish writer.

Kroeber, A.L., *Configurations of Culture Growth, Berkeley*, University of California Press, 1944. Kroeber's basic comparative history, based on the study of patterns of genius.

——*Style and Civilizations*, Cornell University Press, 1957. In which Kroeber discusses other comparative historians and, from an octogenarian's viewpoint, what needs to be done.

——*The Nature of Culture,* University of Chicago Press, 1952. A collection of articles, only a few of which have to do with civilizations. Kroeber's famous discussion of the "Superorganic" is included under this cover.

——*Anthropology,* 2d. ed., Harcourt, Brace, 1948; Harcourt, Brace & World paperback, two vols. Rich in theory, far-reaching in scope, carries anthropological approach into the realm of civilizations.

——*An Anthropologist Looks at History,* Berkeley, University of California Press, 1963. Posthumous publication. A few articles round out or summarize Kroeber's theory.

——*A Roster of Civilizations and Culture,* New York, Viking Fund Publications, 1962. Barely more than an outline of what might have been an important book.

Kroeber and Kluckhohn, *Culture,* New York, Random House, 1952. A demonstration of many approaches to culture, including a consideration of its relation to civilization.

Kuhn, Thomas, *The Structure of Scientific Revolutions,* University of Chicago Press, 1962. Phoenix paperback, 1962. Coulborn felt that the concept of paradigms described here could appropriately be applied to the emerging situation in the comparative study of civilizations.

Mahdi, Mushin, *Ibn Khaldun's Philosophy of History,* London, Allen & Unwin, 1953. An introduction.

Manuel, Frank E., *Shapes of Philosophical History,* Stanford University Press, 1965; Stanford U.P. paperback, 1965. My favorite historiography. His weapon is wit rather than sarcasm, his characterization of several comparative historians, particularly Spengler, is profound (i.e. rather what I would like to have said).

Montagu, M. F. Ashley, ed., *Toynbee and History,* Boston, Porter Sargent, 1956. In contrast to the lovey Allen volume on Sorokin, here the gloves are off. Each critic bows to Toynbee's immense learning, then gleefully tears him to shreds.

Mumford, Lewis, *The Transformations of Man,* New York, Harper, 1956; Collier paperback. Another interpretation of history, like Jaspers, reconciling the narrative and the comparative approaches.

——*The City in History,* New York, Harcourt & Brace, 1961. Though chronologically organized, the book's perspectives are influenced by the author's awareness of comparative history.

Northrop, F.S.C., *The Meeting of East and West,* New York, Macmillan, 1946; Collier paperback, 1946. Well-known example of the view, largely rejected by comparative historians, that a dichotomy exists between Eastern and Western civilizations.

——"The Wedding of the World's Civilizations," *Main Currents in Modern Thought,* May-June 1965, 100-104. A brief, recent example of Northrop's viewpoint, in this case emphasizing signs of a merging of East and West into a world civilization.

Opler, Morris, "The Human Being in Culture Theory," *American Anthropologist,* June 1964, Part I, 507-528. Criticizes Kroeber and others for undervaluing the capacities of human beings.

Petrie, W. M. Flinders, *The Revolutions of Civilisation,* London, Harper, 1911, o.p. An audacious effort that, according to Christopher Dawson, had a tremendous impact on comparative historians writing after World War I.

Prakash, Buddha, *The Modern Approach to History,* Jullundur, University Publishers, 1963.* Herbert Muller observes that it is refreshing to read historical interpretations by one coming from India. Apparently less dogmatic, like most post-World War II writers.

Quigley, Carroll, *The Evolution of Civilizations,* New York, Macmillan, 1961. Graceful, sophisticated, strong on economic theory. The product of seven weeks' writing after thirty years' thinking.

Redfield, Robert, *The Primitive World and its Transformations,* Cornell U. P., 1953. Examines transformation to civilization from primitive viewpoint, emphasizing outlook rather than technology. Charming and provocative.

Reiser, Oliver L., *Cosmic Humanism,* Cambridge, Schenkman, 1966. Though not a comparative historian, Reiser is a pioneer integrative model builder with a tone, spirit and scope rather like Sorokin's. He ranges freely through science, religion and aesthetics.

Roesler, Herbert E., *Table of History of Civilizations*, Bogota, multilith, revised ed., 1968; obtainable from the author at Carrera 16-A, No. 29-18, Bogota, Colombia. A remarkable synthesis of civilization delineations derived from several dozen historians, social scientists and philosophers.

Schweitzer, Albert, *The Decay and the Restoration of Civilization*, London, Black, 1932, 2d edition; translated by Charles Campion. Later published as the first volume of *The Philosophy of Civilization*, New York, Macmillan, paperback, 1949. Stresses and deprecates the unique aspects of Western civilization.

Smith, Page, *The Historian and History*, New York, Knopf, 1964; Vintage paperbacks. Relates some comparative historians — Burckhardt, Spengler, Toynbee — to others pursuing major problems. Treatment is compressed but judicious.

Sorokin, Pitirim A., *Social and Cultural Dynamics*, American Book Company, 1937-41, four volumes. Revised and abridged by the author in one volume, Boston, Porter Sargent, 1957. Though Sorokin would have protested, the abridged volume is adequate for straight reading, while the original may be reserved as a valuable source of statistics to support research.

——*Society, Culture and Personality*, New York, Harper, 1947. Individual chapters supplement *Dynamics*. More oriented toward the contemporary world.

——*Social Philosophies of an Age of Crisis*, London, Stevens & Sons, 1950; in paperback as *Modern Historical and Social Philosophies*, Dover, 1964. The first significant recognition of the existence of a school of comparative historians.

——*Sociological Theories of Today*, New York, Harper & Row, 1966. Part Three: "Theories of Cultural Systems" modifies and adds to Sorokin's earlier *Social Philosophies*.

Spengler, Oswald, *The Decline of the West*, London, Allen and Unwin, 1932, one-volume edition; translated by C. F. Atkinson. Still, despite its overstatement, one of the most seminal comparative histories.

——*Man and Technics*, London, Allen & Unwin, 1932, translated by Atkinson. A minor supplement.

Steward, Julian H., *Theory of Culture Change*, University of Illinois Press, 1955. Includes civilization among cultures.

Moves rapidly, assumes considerable familiarity with anthropology and history.

Thompson, Kenneth, "Mr. Toynbee and World Politics," *World Politics,* VIII: 374-392. A convenient and rather gentle assessment of Toynbee's contribution to the study of international relations.

Toynbee, Arnold J., *A Study of History,* London and New York, Milford and Oxford University Press, 1934-61; O.U.P. paperback; twelve volumes: first ten abridged by D. C. Somervell, London, New York, Cumberlege and Oxford, 1946-57; Dell paperbacks. The abridgement imposes order but misses many of Toynbee's most valuable insights, which usually come when he is wandering from the point.

——*Civilization on Trial,* London, Cumberlege, 1948, o.p.; Meridian paperback, o.p.

——*The Prospects of Western Civilization,* New York, Columbia University Press, 1949; Meridian paperback. Both books are restatements of material carried in the *Study.*

——*An Historian's Approach to Religion,* London, Cumberlege, 1956. Only marginally relevant to comparative history.

——*The New Opportunity for Historians,* University of Minnesota Press, 1956. On the relationship of comparative and narrative history.

——*The Tragedy of Greece,* Oxford, Clarendon Press, 1921. Interesting because it foreshadows Toynbee's theory in a lecture given before he had read Spengler.

Tuma, Elias H., *Twenty-six Years of Agrarian Reform,* University of California Press, 1965.* He uses an approach that may recur frequently in the next couple of decades: a historical survey followed by a comparative analysis and concluded with an attempt at a general theory.

Vico, Giambattista, *The New Science of Giambattista Vico,* Cornell University Press, 1948, o.p.; Anchor paperback, o.p.; translated by Thomas Bergin and Max Fisch. The translators have simplified Vico's style, but it is still a chore to push through. See *Croce.*

Warner, Sam Bass, Jr., "If All the World Were Philadelphia," *American Historical Review,* October, 1968, 26-43. An attempt to set up for the comparative study of cities by selecting meaningful static periods and isolating data on social and economic patterns.

Webb, Walter Prescott, *The Great Frontier,* University of Texas
   Press, 1964. Introduction by Toynbee. A study of the relation between barbarian and civilization since the beginning
   of the expansion of modern Europe.
Wesson, Robert G., *The Imperial Order,* University of California Press, 1967. Studies empires from the Old Kingdom
   through Russia. Writes crisply with less dogmatism than
   Wittfogel and greater clarity than Eisenstadt.
Wittfogel, Karl A., *Oriental Despotism,* Yale University Press,
   1957; Yale U.P. paperback, 1957. A controversial comparative study of despotic power and its relationships to such
   phenomena as property, classes, psychic response and transis-
   tion.
Wright, Quincy, *A Study of War,* University of Chicago Press,
   1942, two volumes. Vies with Sorokin as a source of information, but is too encompassing, lacks point of view, tends
   to be stodgy.
Zimmerman, Carle C., *Patterns of Social Change,* Washington,
   Public Affairs Press, 1956. Much of this essay is devoted to
   the contribution of Spengler, Toynbee and Sorokin toward
   the reshaping of the study of sociology.

2: Topical Listing

In subsections A, B, and C, below, I have listed the more important comparative studies. Section D concerns culture theory;
E, background, explanation and criticism; F, comparative histories
of historical interest. The books in section A are listed in order
of publication, those in the other sections roughly in order of
relevance to this particular study.

From time to time I have been asked which comparative historian should be read first. With the warning that comparative
history is no substitute for narrative history, and assuming a
long life, I have listed a suggested order in section G.

A. Basic Comparative Histories
Spengler, *The Decline of the West*
Toynbee, *A Study of History*
Sorokin, *Social and Cultural Dynamics*

Kroeber, *Configurations of Culture Growth*
Quigley, *The Evolution of Civilizations*

B.   IMPORTANT COMPARATIVE STUDIES OF PARTICULAR SUBJECTS

Coulborn, *The Origin of Civilized Societies*
Coulborn and others, *Feudalism in History*
Clough, *The Rise and Fall of Civilization*
Wright, *A Study of War*
Wesson, *The Imperial Order*
Eisenstadt, *The Political System of Empires*
Wittfogel, *Oriental Despotism*
Webb, *The Great Frontier*
Black, *The Dynamics of Modernization*
Kann, *The Problem of Restoration*
Brinton, *The Anatomy of Revolution*
Benedict, *Patterns of Culture*
Adams, *The Evolution of Urban Society*
Grant, *Ancient History*

C.   OTHER USEFUL SOURCES OF COMPARATIVE THEORY

Dawson, *The Dynamics of World History*
Sorokin, *Society, Culture and Personality*
Kroeber, *Anthropology*
Kroeber, *The Nature of Culture*
Jaspers, *The Origin and Goal of History*
Mumford, *The Transformations of Man*
Bagby, *Culture and History*
Berdyaev, *The Meaning of History*
Schweitzer, *The Decay and the Restoration of Civilization*

D.   CULTURE THEORY

Kroeber, *The Nature of Culture*
Coulborn, *The Origin of Civilized Societies*
Dawson, *The Dynamics of World History*
Redfield, *The Primitive World and its Transformations*
Steward, *Theory of Culture Change*
Benedict, *Patterns of Culture*
Kluckhohn, "The Concept of Culture"
Kroeber and Kluckhohn, *Culture*
Sorokin, *Society, Culture and Personality*
Bagby, *Culture and History*
Herskovits, *Man and His Works*

Coulborn, "Survival of the Fittest in the Atomic Age"
Opler, "The Human Being in Culture Theory"
Bagby, "Culture and the Causes of Culture"

E. CRITICISM

Sorokin, *Social Philosophies of an Age of Crisis*
Kroeber, *Style and Civilizations*
Sorokin, *Sociological Theories of Today*
Manuel, *Shapes of Philosophical History*
Dawson, *Dynamics of World History*
Hughes, *Oswald Spengler*
Toynbee, *Reconsiderations* (Vol. XII of *A Study of History*)
Coulborn, "Toynbee's Reconsiderations"
Coulborn and Du Bois, "Mr. Sorokin's Systems"
Ashley Montagu, *Toynbee and History*
Thompson, "Mr. Toynbee and World Politics"
Geyl, *Debates with Historians*
Collingwood, *The Idea of History*
Smith, *The Historian and History*
Opler, "The Human Being in Culture Theory"
Black, *The Dynamics of Modernization*
Zimmerman, *Patterns of Social Change*
Allen, *Pitirim A. Sorokin in Review*

F. OF HISTORICAL INTEREST

Petrie, *The Revolutions of Civilisation*
Burckhardt, *Force and Freedom*
Sorokin, *Social Philosophies of an Age of Crisis* (the chapter on Danilevsky)
Adams, Brooks, *The Law of Civilization and Decay*
Adams, Henry, *The Degradation of the Democratic Dogma*
Croce, *The Philosophy of Giambattista Vico*
Vico, *The New Science*
Mahdi, *Ibn Khaldun's Philosophy of History*
Ibn Khaldun, *The Muqaddimah*
Bodin, *Method for the Easy Comprehension of History*

G. SUGGESTED ORDER FOR BEGINNING A STUDY OF COMPARATIVE HISTORY

Quigley, *Evolution of Civilizations*. Readable, sophisticated, compact.

Kroeber, *Style and Civilizations.* A brief introduction to comparative historical method, to the historians themselves and to the problems that have to be tackled.

Spengler, *The Decline of the West.* Now you are on the high road. Chapter II of Volume I may be skipped with profit.

Kroeber, *Configurations of Culture Growth.* Kroeber's major book. His caution and kindness contrast with Spengler's arrogant dogmatism.

Sorokin, *Social and Cultural Dynamics,* abridged edition. This will be tough going in places, but worth the effort.

Coulborn, *The Origin of Civilized Societies.* Important for original views of civilization as well as detective-story theory of origins.

Redfield, *The Primitive World and its Transformations.* Tackles Coulborn's problem from the viewpoint of the primitive culture rather than the civilization.

Grant, *Ancient History.* Singles out a few major topics for generalization at the civilized level.

Mumford, *The Transformations of Man.* Argues for a significant differentiation between the kind of civilizations Grant studies and the civilization of the past few hundred years.

Toynbee, *A Study of History,* Volumes I-IX. The Somervell abridgement is an inadequate substitute. The original makes good bedtime reading. Allow two years of evenings and don't shortchange the footnotes and annexes. Probably should be reread every thirty or forty years.

INDEX

OTHER EXTENDING HORIZONS BOOKS

SOCIAL AND CULTURAL DYNAMICS by Pitirim A. Sorokin, 1957. 718 pp. $10. SBN 87558-029-7. The late founder of Harvard's sociology department made his own 1-vol. abridgement of his major 4-vol. work of research into Western cultural and social trends. In it he lays down the empirical basis for his new sociology of values and his cyclical theory of social change.

POWER AND MORALITY by Pitirim A. Sorokin & Walter Lunden. 1959. 204 pp. $3.50 SBN 87558-032-7. This·book presents a challenge to both rulers and ruled that is particularly urgent at the present time: to discard the weapons we have invented in our fear of each other, and to welcome a new kind of government based on scientific knowledge, wisdom and creative love.

TOYNBEE AND HISTORY, ed. M. F. Ashley Montagu. 1956. 385 pp. $5. SBN 87558-026-2. Critical evaluations of **A Study of History** by 29 distinguished scholars, introduced by Ashley Montagu.

ANTHROPOLOGY AND HUMAN NATURE by M. F. Ashley Montagu. 1957. 390 pp. $6. SBN 87558-030-3. The theme of these essays is that anthropology is the bridge between the sciences and the humanities. Topics discussed include human nature, race, medicine, sexual development, crime. Complete bibliography of Montagu's anthropological writings.

MUTUAL AID by Petr Kropotkin. 1955 400 pp. $4 cloth; $2 paper. SBN 87558-023-8/024-6. In this classic work a major anarchist thinker provides new insights into the "survival of the fittest" theory and its distortions by social theorists. In particular he answers T. H. Huxley's famous essay, "The Struggle for Existence" here reprinted. Includes Preface to 1914 edition. Foreward by Ashley Montagu.

DIALECTICAL SOCIOLOGY by Phillip Bosserman. 1968. 336 pp. $7.95. SBN 87558-040-8. Bosserman introduces Americans to the work of the eminent French sociologist, Georges Gurvitch. He sought to combine the fields of sociology, history and philosophy by his dialectical method, and explored the process of change with an eye to stimulating rapid reform, rather than control. Foreward by Sorokin.

PORTER SARGENT PUBLISHER
11 Beacon Street   Boston Mass. 02108

DATE